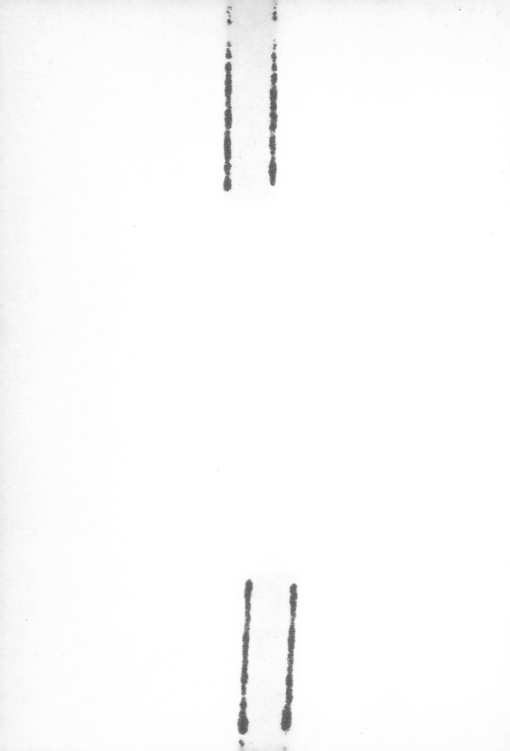

TRAINS

This book tries to show something of how the railroads were born and grew to their present state, the work they can do today, the way they do it and the shape they may take in the future. Railroads and trains, like trucks and cars and roads, ships and the sea, aircraft and the air, are means of transport. Though some people may love them for the shape of a locomotive boiler or the carving on an old station wall, railroads will only survive if they continue to earn their living. The author believes they *will* survive, even if they are so transformed as to be scarcely recognizable.

The illustrations for this book have been based partly on photographic and other material gathered by the author over a long period of time and partly on the material newly supplied to the publisher and artist. We acknowledge here the help given us by railroad administrations and railroad suppliers in the preparation of this book. The author thanks them also for their general assistance over many years.

A GROSSET
ALL-COLOR GUIDE
TRAINS

BY JOHN DAY

Illustrated by David A. Warner
and Nigel W. Hearn

GROSSET & DUNLAP
A NATIONAL GENERAL COMPANY
Publishers • New York

CONTENTS

How and Why the Railroads Came

Railroads are positively the greatest blessing that the ages have wrought out for us.

Nathaniel Hawthorne

No one knows just how — or when — the first railroad was built. Like the wheel, its origins are lost in time. Perhaps the parallel lines of grooved stone blocks laid by the Greeks to move ships across the Isthmus of Corinth some 2,500 years ago were the first railroads. They were a special form of road for a special type of vehicle, they were self-guiding and permanent, and they moved both people and goods.

For our purposes we have to look back some 400 years to the days of Queen Elizabeth I. At that time we know that men in Alsace were moving coal from the mine faces of Leberthal in small trucks with flanged wheels running on timber rails. Such a wagon, from a Transylvanian gold mine, with a piece of track and even points, is still preserved in the Verkehrs und Bau Museum in Berlin.

The mines of northern England brought the railroads to

Loaded coal wagon coasting downhill. The horse will haul it back.

4

Early 'horse locomotive' with the
horse turning a treadmill.

Great Britain—almost certainly before the sixteenth century
was over. The mine railroads spread, and in 1676 Roger North
was able to describe how coal was carried from the mines to
the rivers by 'bulky carts . . . made with four rowlets fitting
these rails'. On these straight and parallel tracks of timber, he
explained, one horse could 'draw four or five chaldrons of
coals'.

The secret of the rails, a secret which they keep to this
day, is that on them a given tractive force can do far more
work than it could on any non-specialized road.

Wooden rails wore out quickly, so that when iron became
cheaper and more easily worked it was natural that cast plates
should be nailed over the rails to make them last longer. Angle
plates were laid at Sheffield, England in 1776, with the wheels
running on the flat part and the raised angle preventing the
wheels from leaving the track. Any ordinary cart with suitable
wheel spacing could use these tracks, and as the usual spacing
was a little less than five feet this became standard. In this
manner grew up the 'standard' gauge of 4 feet 8½ inches used

by many railroads throughout the world.

The first rails resembling those of today came in 1789, when William Jessop, engineer of a line near Loughborough, laid his own design of cast iron rails. These first rails were very short — about three feet each — and easily broken, but they were the model from which the rails of today have grown.

When, in England, the Surrey Iron Railway, the first public freight railroad in the world to be sanctioned by a government, opened in 1803 a test was made to see how much a single horse could draw. It started off with twelve wagons, each weighing three tons, and other wagons were added at each stop. At the end of the six-mile journey the horse was pulling a fifty-five-ton train with fifty people on top of the load.

The speed of a horse walking over the sleepers between the rails was not very great, so the idea was born that the horse might be carried in the train while at the same time driving it through a form of treadmill. The first 'horse locomotives' of any practical value appeared just at the time when the steam locomotive was proving its mettle. One of them, the *Cycloped*, patented by Thomas Shaw Brandreth, was a direct competitor of the *Rocket* at the historical Rainhill trials in 1829. This machine had two horses but seems to have been too crudely built to give the horses a fair chance.

A better impression can be gained from trials on the South Carolina Railroad in 1830. Using a horse which the *Charleston Courier* described as 'very inferior in action and power', a twelve-passenger car built by Messrs. Dotterer & Detmold ran 2½ miles at just over 9 m.p.h. and back again to over 12 m.p.h.

Even in the 1850's, when the steam locomotive was firmly established, an intricate, geared, horse locomotive was demonstrated in Britain, France and Germany. A two-horse version

6

A horse train in the
1820's.

Early railroad sailing car on the
Baltimore & Ohio Railroad

7

Richard Trevithick's *Catch-me-who-can* near Euston Road, London.

hauled thirty wagons in trials at Nine Elms, London, in 1850 and a four-horse type was shown in Berlin in 1853.

An even cheaper—if less reliable—method of powering trains was tried in the United States in 1830. The Baltimore & Ohio's sailing car *Aeolus* made its maiden voyage in charge of a sailing-master from Chesapeake Bay. Four days later she set off again carrying the eminent engineer DeWitt Clinton. With a good breeze she glided along at a fast clip, but when they came to the end of the track the sailing-master forgot to

apply the brakes, and she ran into a mud bank. The South
Carolina Railroad tried a sailing car two months later. Loaded
with three tons of iron ballast and fifteen people, it lost its
mast in a gust of wind while making nearly twelve knots on its
trial run.

The first steam locomotive to haul a load along a railroad
came in 1804. It was the work of a remarkable Englishman,
Richard Trevithick, who had built and demonstrated a steam
road engine—known locally as 'Captain Dick's Puffer'—three
years before and had designed a locomotive for the Coal-
brookdale Iron Works in 1803. This locomotive was never
built, but the 1804 machine was probably very much like it,
with one large cylinder and a huge flywheel. It had no flanges
on its four wheels, for it ran on the nine-mile flanged plateway
at the Penydarren Iron Works where it easily hauled a twenty-
five-ton load. Another locomotive built by Trevithick and
John Steele, in 1805 for the Wylam Colliery had flanged
wheels to run on wooden rails.

In 1808 Trevithick made his mark in London with a neat
little eight-ton locomotive that he put to work on a circular
track of iron rails in an enclosure where for a shilling the
public could watch or ride in a converted carriage drawn—at up
to 12 m.p.h.—by the engine. The engine was labeled 'Catch-
me-who-can', and thousands did catch it until a rail broke
and the locomotive overturned, ending the career of London's

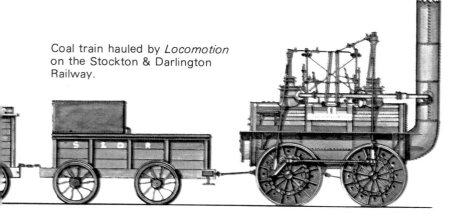

Coal train hauled by *Locomotion*
on the Stockton & Darlington
Railway.

first steam railroad and of Trevithick's interest in the locomotive. He was the true father of the locomotive, pioneering such features as the use of high-pressure steam, the turning of the exhaust steam into the chimney to improve the draft in the firebox, and the return flue boiler. He also demonstrated that smooth wheels would haul a load on a smooth track.

Another Englishman, George Stephenson, obtained funds to build an edge-rail locomotive with smooth wheels for

The Stephenson *Rocket,* victor of the Rainhill locomotive trials.

The age of steam arrives. Trains like these were to open up travel for all in the next few decades.

The Killingworth Coalwork, the first smooth-wheel engine to run on iron edge-rails. Other successful Stephenson locomotives followed until, with the *Locomotion*, he brought steam to a public railroad.

George Stephenson was appointed Engineer of the Stockton & Darlington Railway in 1822, and an act of 1823 gave the railroad powers both to carry passengers and to use steam locomotives. For the opening on September 27, 1825, George Stephenson and his son Robert built the four-wheeled, eight-ton *Locomotion*. According to contemporary accounts, the ninety-ton inaugural train, with George Stephenson on the footplate, reached 15 m.p.h. After the opening day the Stockton & Darlington used horses for passenger trains and kept the locomotives for coal traffic.

In the next few years locomotives were built by the Stephensons, Timothy Hackworth, Robert Wilson and others, but the great flowering of the steam age came in 1830.

After a survey of existing railroads, the directors of the Liverpool & Manchester Railway, then under construction, offered a prize of £ 500 for the best locomotive engine to meet specific conditions. Five machines were ready for the trials when they began on October 6, 1829. Timothy Burstall's *Perseverance* and the *Cycloped* (already mentioned) failed to reach the required speed and Timothy Hackworth's *Sans Pareil* was over the weight limit. This left the *Rocket* and Braithwaite's and Ericsson's *Novelty*, the popular favorite

11

that broke down on both days of its trials. The *Rocket,* by George and Robert Stephenson and Henry Booth, survived all the tests and reached 24.1 m.p.h. with full load, as well as 29 m.p.h. running light. It was awarded the prize and, more important, ensured that steam would work the new railroad.

On September 15, 1830, the railroad era began with the opening of the Liverpool & Manchester — the first public railroad in the world to be worked entirely by steam locomotives. The glory of the occasion was marred by the first accident on a public railroad, when William Huskisson, a Member of Parliament and a good friend of the railroad, was run down by the

The *Best Friend of Charleston,* 1830.

The *Münchner,* an 1841
German-built locomotive.

Rocket. He died the same night. So began the Railroad
Age in a mixture of triumph and tragedy.

Meanwhile, engineers elsewhere were following up, the
lead established in Great Britain. America's first steam railroad was a circular track built on the lawn of Colonel John
Stevens' house in Hoboken, New Jersey, on which in 1825
ran a small locomotive built by the seventy-five-year-old
Colonel. Next came the *Stourbridge Lion,* imported from England in 1829, and in August 1830 the *Tom Thumb,* built
by Peter Cooper of New York. Cooper's engine was really a
demonstration model designed to persuade the United States
businessmen that steam locomotion was a practical thing.
The first steam locomotive to run in regular service in the
United States was the *Best Friend of Charleston* on the South
Carolina Railroad in 1830.

Marc Seguin built the first French locomotive in 1829, and
in Germany, the first public railroad was opened in 1835
between Nuremberg and Fürth. Using a locomotive from
the Robert Stephenson works in England, *Le Beuth,* designed
and built by August Borsig in Berlin in 1841, was one of the
first German-built engines. In the same year the Maffei works
built its first *Münchner.*

13

Building the early railroads.
Civil engineers took on new and
gigantic tasks.

14

The first Pullman cars introduced in Britain in the 1870's were American in appearance and design.

The railroad mania was on. Parliament was impossibly overwhelmed with railroad bills—more than 470 were being considered early in April 1846 and 272 acts were passed in that year. Very often there was no money to build the authorized lines, and some promoters obtained acts only to keep others out of 'their' territory. Of the lines authorized in 1846 more than 4,500 miles were built (including some lines in Ireland), but the failure of many companies and the collapse of many railroad shares brought sense to promoters and investors alike. In 1847 only 1,300 miles of line were authorized. The 1850's were largely devoted to building and linking railroads already in existence, but a new upsurge of activity began in the 1860's, during which time 4,500 miles of railroad were added.

In spite of the fact that Europe had better engineering techniques during this early period, by 1840 the United States had 3,000 miles of new road, while in all of Europe there were only 1,800 miles. In addition, the invested sum of about $80 million was far less than that spent in Europe for its less extensive systems.

A national sense of urgency, to quote Calhoun, " . . . to bind the republic together with a perfect system of roads and canals" together with a freedom from a multitude of customs and prejudices was largely responsible for this expansion.

Railroads became an important factor in the Civil War, beginning in 1861. The trains served to transport troops and arms to both training areas and fighting fronts. Both North and South worked to capture or destroy the other's supply lines. The War slowed but did not stop railroad expansion, and after the War tracks were laid very rapidly, employing the labor of many ex-soldiers.

To promote western expansion, the United States government began to offer land grants to railroads from 1850, the first being to the Illinois Central Railroad. From 2,800 miles of railroad in 1840, the United States systems grew to 9,000 miles in 1850, 30,000 in 1860, and 53,000 in 1870. Railroad empires and emperors sprang up and prospered. Many of the lines were lightly laid over flat, easy land, with bogie locomotives and vehicles used to spread the weight over more wheels, but the distance over which the rails spread is astonishing. The long runs meant that there had to be facilities for moving about in the train, for eating and sleeping, so the open car with end platforms became the rule. By 1859 George Mortimer Pullman had produced a sleeping car conversion, a sleeping car built for the purpose by 1865 and an eating and sleeping car

Liverpool & Manchester
Railway coach.

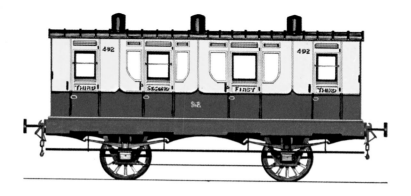

An early Great Western Railroad coach and an open-topped third-class coach as used on the Liverpool & Manchester.

by 1867 (for a Canadian railroad). East and West were linked on May 10, 1869, when the Union Pacific and the Central Pacific Railroads met at Promontory, Utah. A golden spike was driven to complete the rail connections and the sound of the hammer blows was carried by telegraph across the width of the continent.

In Europe, British engineers, contractors and locomotives were prominent in the birth of steam railroads. Robert Stephenson was active in Belgium (where his father was engineer to the first railroad), in Denmark, Sweden, Switzerland, Egypt and elsewhere. Early Stephenson locomotives went even further afield, to Belgium, Germany, France, Russia, Austria and Italy, for example, as well as to the United States. Thomas Brassey, using local labor spearheaded by some of his 'navvies' from Britain, managed contracts in many European countries, and also in South America, India, Australia and Canada.

The first Belgian railroad, opened between Brussels and Malines in 1835, is notable as having been promoted, paid for and worked by the Government as part of a planned national system. The first German railroad opened later the same year. A Canadian line between Laprairie and St. John followed in 1836. All three railroads had Stephenson locomotives. The St. Etienne — Andrézieux Railroad, the first in France, opened in 1828, but it did not carry passenger traffic until 1832. These railroads were all later than one in the old Austrian Empire. It ran the eight miles from Budweis to Trojanov, and when it opened, with horse traction, on September 7, 1827, it was almost certainly the first in Europe.

The Dutch opened a line between Amsterdam and Haarlem, and the Italians opened a line between Naples and Portici, in 1839. The Spanish decided in 1844 that they would use a five-foot six-inch gauge and opened their first line, between Barcelona and Mataró, to this gauge in 1848. Russia was early in the field with the six-foot gauge. Petersburg & Pavlovsk Railroad opened from Pavlovsk to Tsarskoye Selo in 1836 and the 400-mile, almost straight St. Petersburg — Moscow railroad begun on the five-foot gauge in 1843 and opened throughout in 1851. Switzerland and Denmark, with first lines in 1847, were late on the railroad scene, with Norway (1854) and Sweden (1856) still later.

Under British influence, an Indian railroad was opened between Bombay and Thana in 1853, (5 foot 6 inch gauge) and the first Australian railroad to carry passengers and goods opened with horse traction in South Australia in May 1854, followed by a steam line, between Flinders Street and Port Melbourne, in Victoria. There were nearly 128,000 miles of railroad for public use in the world by 1870.

Quite apart from the obvious advantages of the railroad in providing quick and cheap passenger travel and freeing industry from the need to be situated either near its main market or its source of raw materials, there were incidental benefits. News spread quickly and mails were speeded up as the Post Office took advantage of the new form of transport. The telegraph, the first reliable method of sending instantaneous messages, grew up alongside the railroad and was used largely for railroad purposes. Railroad timetables demanded uniform timekeeping instead of local time, so railroad, and afterward all other clocks, were synchronized on Greenwich time. As men traveled they took their thoughts, their ideas, their manner of speech with them.

Another effect was that the more wealthy were able to live further from their work, causing a movement away from the center of the cities to the suburbs. The vacated houses were often taken over, as time went on, by poor families, and the rows of fashionable houses often degenerated to slums.

The effect on cities was multiplied by the growth of urban, as distinct from suburban, railroads. It is remarkable to consider that London had steam locomotives operating in a metro under-ground system before the first tracks met across the vast expanse of the United States.

Telegraph Cottage,
Slough, on the Great
Western Railroad, 1844

The Railroad Age

For the world as a whole, the year 1870 might mark the beginning of the Railroad Age. By then the United States had some 53,000 miles of road, but railroads had been big business since as early as 1850. The total investment in the industry more than tripled in the ensuing decade, amounting to one and a half billion dollars by 1860.

In 1870 the British railroad map was not unlike that of today, consisting of about 13,500 miles of track. There were no railroads in China or Japan, or in most of Africa except the far north and far south. Great railroad networks such as those of Argentina, Brazil and Mexico, and smaller ones—Chile, Paraguay, Peru, and Uruguay—in South and Central America, were just taking their first tentative steps toward expansion. Four Australian states were in the Railroad Age, the others were not, but New Zealand had a foot, though no more than that, in the doorway. Most of Europe was not far behind Britain, but Canada's 2,000 miles of track was only one-twentieth of her eventual limit.

While the late-comers were building or developing railroads on foundations already well established elsewhere, the main stream of progress was leading to faster, more comfortable trains for passengers and better service for freight. Steam was still king and was to reign for many more years, but in 1879, a miniature four-wheeled electric locomotive built by Werner von Siemens was seen hauling up to thirty people at a time around a narrow-gauge track in the grounds of

Early American type of
wood-burning locomotive.

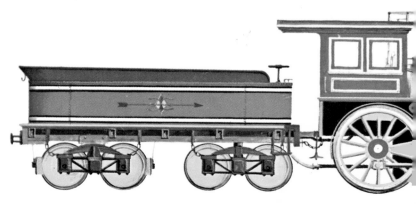

Chicago & Atlantic Railroad station in the early days when two Pullman car trains a day ran between Chicago and New York.

the Berlin Trades Exhibition. Though so small that the driver straddled it as though it were a horse, it was the first practicable electric locomotive and picked up its power from the track just as electric trains do today. Only four years later, on August 3, 1883, Britain's first electric railroad opened. This line, which still exists, in Brighton, was named 'Volk's

Electric Railway' after Magnus Volk, who promoted it as a private venture. In the United States the first main-line electrification was achieved in 1895 on the Baltimore & Ohio Railroad, between Camden, New Jersey and Baltimore, Maryland.

Meanwhile, steam was showing what it could do, and there is no better example of the way improvements in speed were made than the London-Edinburgh 'Race to the North' of 1888. This arose from rivalry between the London & North Western Railway and its partner of the West Coast Route, the Caledonian, and the Great Northern, North Eastern, and North British Railways of the East Coast.

In 1885 the West Coast trains took 10 hours from London, while the East Coast's Flying Scotsman made the same trip in 9 hours. When in 1887 the East Coast line began carrying third-class passengers, the West Coast line soon began losing its own passenger volume. In an attempt to recover, the West Coast line equalled the running time of the East Coast line, which then shortened the trip to 8½ hours. In efforts to out-do each other, the two lines almost daily announced shorter running times, until eventually it was decided that the East Coast route would take 7¾ hours and the West Coast, 8 hours.

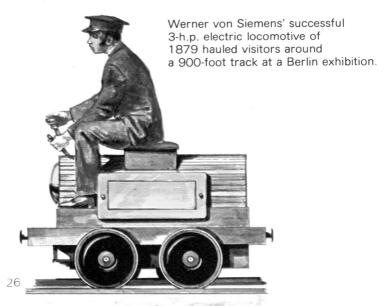

Werner von Siemens' successful
3-h.p. electric locomotive of
1879 hauled visitors around
a 900-foot track at a Berlin exhibition.

This rivalry, followed by newspapers all over the world, was the spur that brought out the best in railroad men and equipment, and showed what could be done in the way of high-speed running.

All the trains involved in these races made a stop for lunch. At Preston, for example, passengers were expected to eat soup, a meat course, a dessert, cheese and biscuits, and coffee and be back in their seats in twenty minutes. But not all trains of the period stopped for meals. As early as 1867 the Great Western Railway of Canada had begun a regular dining car service, using a car built by George Mortimer Pullman. In Britain, sleeping cars were introduced on the East Coast route in July and on the West Coast route in October 1873. American-style Pullman cars appeared on the Midland Railway in 1874; they had buffet bars for refreshments.

Speed rivalries in later years led to better public service

Magnus Volk's electric railroad at Brighton, the first in Britain.

as, for example, the competition between the Pennsylvania Railroad, with its 902-mile, steeply graded route from New York to Washington and the New York Central, with its 'Water Level' route, much flatter but some fifty-six miles longer. The New York Central's *Twentieth Century Limited* and the Pennsylvania's *Broadway Limited* raced on these routes for many years, especially in the 1930's. In 1935, both trains ran the trip in seventeen hours, but already the writing was on the wall for steam. The pioneer streamlined diesel train, the four-car *Pioneer Zephyr* of the Burlington Railroad, had, in 1934, set up an average speed of 77.6 m.p.h. for the 1,015 mile run from Denver to Chicago, and diesel unit trains and locomotives were soon to oust steam, despite efforts to streamline steam locomotives and give them a new look.

Electric locomotives have many advantages. They can be used for both heavy passenger and freight trains; they can accelerate rapidly and make no smoke; they can run either forward or backward with equal efficiency. Also, they are always ready for immediate service since they need not generate fire or steam before they begin their run.

In Europe the great international trains were largely in the hands of the Compagnie Internationale des Wagons-Lits, formed in 1876. The company provided luxurious cars for trains which covered long distances at high speeds. Stops for frontier formalities made very high speeds out of the

question. The *Orient Express,* the first of these famous trains, began running in 1883 between Paris, Vienna and Istanbul, and soon afterward the company added 'et des Grands Express Européens' to its title. The second train was the 'Calais–Nice–Rome Express'. Then came Ostend–Vienna (1894), Paris–St. Petersburg (1895) and many others. The company still operates today and its fine sleeping and dining cars—among the best in the world—can be seen on any trip to Europe. Its cars also offer Pullman-type services on many ordinary trains.

The railroads themselves were still expanding. A start was made on the Pacific coast of Russia in 1891 on a railroad which, at 4,607 miles, was to become the world's longest. This, the Trans-Siberian Railroad, was opened as a through route in 1900, although it then included a considerable journey— about 1,400 miles—by steamer. In 1901 Wagons-Lits cars formed the 'Trans-Siberian Express' from Moscow as far as Irkutsk. The line, now greatly improved, is truly the backbone of the present Russian railroad system.

A Stirling 'single' on the East Coast Route to Scotland.

Early scene on South Africa's three-foot
six-inch gauge railroads.

In Africa, Cecil Rhodes dreamed of a railroad route that
would link Cairo with Cape Town and pass through all
the British possessions in the continent on the way. No through
line exists even now, although the trip is possible with some
railroad steamer trips and a short road journey or two. Air
travel has made the through line unnecessary, but the railroads
on the route were largely responsible for developing the
territories they serve. Egypt's first railroad — a Robert Stephenson line from Alexandria to Cairo — opened in 1856 and South
Africa's first in 1860. Rhodesia's first line, from the junction
with South African lines at the border to Mafeking, opened in
1894. By 1906 the rails had reached Broken Hill, 2,017 miles
from Cape Town. From here the route can be traced through
the Congo, East Africa, and the Sudan to Egypt, but there are
differences of gauge as well as gaps between railheads.

In 1910 the railroads crossed the Andes. The Trans-
Andean line, between Chile and Argentina, reaches 10,515 feet
in the international tunnel through the ridge of the mountains.

30

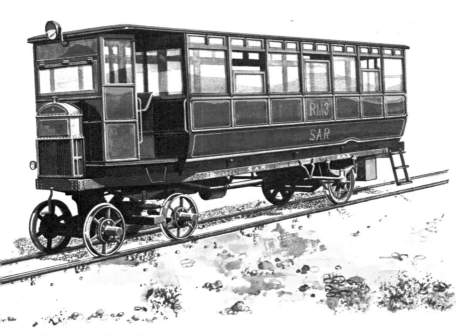

One of the first railcars used on
South African branch lines.

This railroad also suffers from having a different gauge from
the majority of the lines in the two countries it links.

Nowhere is the gauge problem more difficult than in
Australia, where the separate states originally all went their
own way. The Trans-Australian railroad, however, was built
by the Commonwealth Government to connect the rail system
of South Australia with that of Western Australia, formerly
completely isolated. It was built to the standard gauge
(different from both the systems it links) and its 1,050 miles
include some 800 through waterless country. It runs 330 miles
in a straight line over the Nullarbor Plain. Now Australia is
tackling its gauge problem vigorously and providing new
standard-gauge connections.

Wherever the railroads went, travel and trade followed and
grew. Sometimes they opened up remote territories, such as
the American West, sometimes they traversed country already
well served by roads and canals. In the early days the stage
coaches tried hard to compete with the new railroads and in the

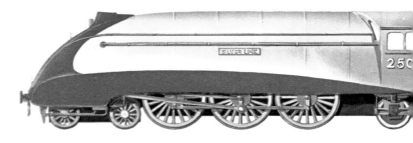

late 1830's, at their peak, they gave a remarkably efficient service. The growing speed of the railroads beat them and their era of prosperity ended—quite quickly—as the railroad trunk lines opened in turn. The canals lasted longer, because an efficient canal had, and still has, some advantages for heavy traffic when time is not important, but for most goods railroad transport soon proved more efficient, especially where the narrow canals were concerned.

War usually results in the running down of railroads in the combatant countries—from wear and lack of maintenance as much as or more than through enemy action. Where they are really badly damaged, as in France in 1939–45, it can be a spur to postwar rebuilding with the latest equipment and result in a much improved system.

Apart from their role in carrying vital war materials in addition to their normal loads, railroads can actually be instruments of military strategy. Light, narrow-gauge railroads have been hastily built to carry troops and their supplies almost into the front lines. A railroad is almost essential as the supply route for an army in action, for nothing else can carry the load for long. The first railroad laid especially for army support was that in the Crimea, from Balaklava to the front line near Sebastopol in 1855.

It was the American Civil War which proved the importance of railroads. They kept the armies of the North, far from their bases, supplied with food, weapons and ammunition. General Sherman's famous march through Georgia 'from Atlanta to the sea' was made possible by the railroad stretching out behind him. It served the troops just as the Desert Railroad stretching out from Egypt along the northern coast of Africa supplied the British Eighth Army in World War II.

One of Gresley's famous
prewar streamlined
'Pacifics'.

Armored car used to
protect repair crews
during the American Civil
War.

Trains for People

Railroads everywhere are engaged in a war—a grim economic war—and in no field is it fiercer than in the battle for passengers. When the railroads came, they generated a demand for travel. The man who might never have moved out of his native region could now afford to travel fifty, a hundred miles, and the speed of railroads gave him time to do it. Now the automobile has brought an even bigger boom in personal travel, and the railroads, in their turn, are fighting a rearguard action in the same way as the stage coaches and canals did in the last century.

The car owner does not think about the cost of his vehicle, the depreciation, maintenance, insurance, taxation and the other payments involved in owning it. When he wants to travel he considers only the cost of his gasoline—the other sums have to be paid whether he uses his car or not—and naturally he regards the car as cheaper than any form of public transport, especially if he has his family with him, and much more convenient because it will take him and his luggage from door to door. Motorcycle and scooter owners think the same. Are the railroads then, to be left with those too young, too old or too poor to have their own transport?

In some places, especially in the United States, some railroads have already reached the stage of dropping passenger service altogether, but there is a special reason for this. Where distances are long, the speed of air travel is such that people will fly rather than undertake a long, comparatively slow drive. Although a train journey would relieve them of fatigue, the speed is still far less than that of an airplane. So the railroad is beset on all sides—by the car for short journeys and the airliner for long.

Fortunately for railroads there is a middle distance at which they are beginning to show they can excel. If speed can be raised enough, the advantage over the car becomes sufficient for business travelers—but not whole families traveling for pleasure. The convenience of the car is still attractive enough for it to be preferred for journeys up to, perhaps, 100 miles. The exact figure depends on the frequency and speed of the train service and the type of road available, but 100 miles is a good round figure. Similarly, the inconvenient situation of most big city airports, involving perhaps an hour's journey by road at each end of the flight, reduces the speed advantage of air travel over journeys of, say, 300 miles — again a very round figure. Somewhere in this middle zone lie journeys for which the railroads have the chance to win patronage. They are now concentrating their efforts in this area.

In Europe, where many journeys between big commercial cities are of suitable length, train travel is still very popular — even booming. In the United States, where distances are greater, passenger traffic is still in a poor way.

The need for speed and for comfort is recognized. Passengers expect comfortable seats, refreshment provisions and washing and toilet facilities. On the more important trains

Electrically hauled train on the London-Liverpool-Manchester route.

they expect—at a somewhat higher fare—to travel in luxury. Such trains are the Trans-Europ Expresses, a series of fast business trains linking 100 or so important commercial cities of Europe and running at speeds that equal or beat air travel for city-center to city-center journeys.

At first these trains were powered by diesel engines so that there would be no difficulties with different forms of electrification in different countries, but now engineers can build electric trains able to run on three or four different systems and many of the new trains are electrically powered. The cars are soundproofed, often air conditioned and have compartments for customs staff so that the trains need not stop at borders. Originally all the trains were international, but recently a few other trains built and operated to the same high standards—like the French *Mistral*—have been allowed to use the title.

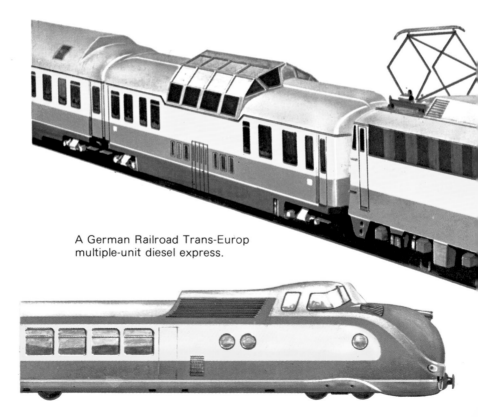

A German Railroad Trans-Europ
multiple-unit diesel express.

All passengers are guaranteed a seat on these trains. A reservation system linked throughout Europe ensures that no ticket is sold unless a seat is available. The timetables are carefully arranged to suit the business man, being designed on the principle that he should be able to travel, have time to transact business at his destination, and return home on the same day. Here, in fact, is a service which started out by considering first what the customer needed instead of what was convenient for the railroad. The reward has been spectacular success.

Many other business trains in Europe are timed with the need for one-day round trips in mind. For example, leaving Paris at 8 a.m., the business man can be in Strasbourg, 313 miles away, at 12:05 in time for a business lunch. Leaving Strasbourg at 7 p.m., he can be back in Paris four hours later. Many business trains have telephones through which the

The German *Rheinpfeil* electrically hauled express with observation dome.

French electric locomotive for Paris-Amsterdam expresses.

Impression of an electric train for the New York-Washington run.
Power is picked up from an overhead line.

traveler can contact office or home. Some have hairdressing salons or secretaries who will deal with urgent business correspondence in any of several languages.

An example of good high-speed passenger services is that of the recently electrified lines between Euston, Manchester and Liverpool in Great Britain. The domestic airlines freely admit that some former air passengers have gone back to the trains, and the air services have been cut. And trains are getting even faster. Many railroads have 125 m.p.h. in mind as a suitable express speed. For example, in May 1967 the French *Capitole,* running the 443 miles between Paris and Toulouse in six hours, was timed to cover the 43½ miles between Les Aubrais and Vierzon at 125 m.p.h. Even so, the Paris–Marseilles *Mistral*—twice its weight—maintains a slightly higher average speed—75 m.p.h. against about 74 m.p.h.

In Japan even higher speeds are reached on the New Tokaido line, a new railroad especially built with all the latest techniques for fast running. This line is being extended to give a

425-mile run from Tokyo to Okayama which the trains will cover, including stops, in 250 minutes—102 m.p.h. Top speeds on the present Tokyo—Osaka section are about 115 m.p.h., but the trains have run up to 150 m.p.h. or so in trials.

In the United States, where rail passenger traffic was once considered lost forever, there is a remarkable renaissance of interest in high-speed rail services. The main target, with help from government funds, is the heavily populated 'corridor' running southward from Boston through New York and Philadelphia to Washington. The Metroliner, Pennsylvania Railroad's new high-speed electric train, reaches 125 m.p.h. in regular service and covers the 228 miles between New York and Washington in less than three hours. It has reached 156 m.p.h. in trials. These trains run on tracks already heavily used by ordinary trains. The United States is also experimenting with fast turbine-powered trains, and Canada recently built similar trains for regular service on the 338-mile Montreal–Toronto run, covered in about four hours. Russia also looks forward to 125 m.p.h. trains in the near future.

New Tokaido Line express at speed in open country.

Double-deck train for commuter traffic in the suburbs of Chicago.

High speeds are possible but expensive. The top speeds achieved with steam before the war were possible only where there was a clear run with other trains kept out of the way for as much as twenty minutes ahead. This safety margin, necessary because the brakes and signalling of the day were not good enough to cope with 100–120 m.p.h. speeds, delayed other trains and therefore cost money.

Today signalling, brakes and track—for the wear on rails rises rapidly with higher speeds—are all being improved at the same time as the motive power; and this too costs money. But modern market research shows that travelers value speed very highly. Some studies, in fact, reveal that an increase in speed of 1 m.p.h. on a journey will result in an increase of at least one percent in traffic. The railroads are left to juggle the costs with the potential profits.

Another point is that fast and (relatively) slow trains cannot be mixed on the same tracks. With 120 m.p.h. passenger trains, 60 m.p.h. freight trains will have to be relegated to the night hours. One only has to draw the simplest of track space/time graphs to see the inordinate amount of track-time occupied by one half-speed train. The alternative is to have one route for passenger trains and another for freight—a solution possible only where a country is over-endowed with railroads. There is still the cost of maintaining two routes instead of one. Perhaps the real solution—a long-term one—is to bring freight trains up to passenger standards. It would certainly cost a lot more for locomotives or other motive power and for rolling stock, but this could show a saving over the years if by ordering and using this advanced equipment it was possible to close down a complete route. Then passenger and freight trains would use the same track, the same signalling, and so on, increasing the volume of use to a point where the equipment could be employed to optimum advantage.

Not all travelers want to cover long distances at high speeds. Many want to travel quite short distances—say five to thirty miles—every working day at the right time to get them from home to their place of work or vice versa. No better way of handling large numbers of people in a short space of time and at a good speed has ever been invented. Over 4½ million people use New York City's mass transit system in a 24-hour

Electric multiple-unit coach for suburban services.

Traveling post office, with net
for picking up mailbags hanging
at the trackside.

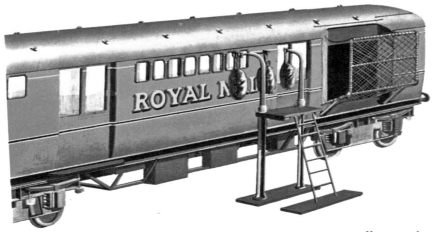

period, and the story is repeated in great cities all over the world. The longer-distance 'commuter' expects a comfortable seat and perhaps breakfast or bar facilities. For medium distances he expects a seat, if nothing else, and much ingenuity has been exercised in designing trains with the greatest number of seats in the space available. In many countries where the height of bridges permits, double-deck trains are used. On very short journeys on suburban routes and on the subways or 'rapid transit' urban railroads, the proportion of seats is small and most commuters stand in peak hours—though the seating is sufficient for the relatively small off-peak traffic.

It is the difference between the demands of traffic in and out of the peaks that makes commuter traffic such a headache for railroads. Many trains are needed only for an hour or two in the morning and the same in the evening. Two sets of train men are needed to cope with two peaks—and the same applies to station and depot staffs, signalmen and so on—they must be at peak efficiency twice a day. Also, more tracks, better signalling, more equipment in general, are needed to handle the twice-a-day peak than would be needed if the traffic could be more evenly spread over a longer period of time.

To get the utmost use out of them, suburban trains are generally of the 'multiple-unit' type with the motors spread out along the train and a driving cab at each end. At the terminal, the driver moves to the other end of the train. The time saved in not having to switch a locomotive from one end to the other is such that in some countries locomotives pull the train in one direction and push it in the other, the driver occupying a specially fitted control compartment built into the end coach.

Passenger trains also carry some high-priority· 'goods' traffic—notably newspapers, mails and parcels. The mails were early railroad passengers—as early as 1834 in the United States—and they have been closely associated with rail travel ever since. One of the most spectacular aspects of this association is the traveling post office, a special car attached to fast trains for the purpose of carrying mail and sorting it en route: the first such car in the United States was placed in service between St. Joseph and Hannibal, Missouri in 1862. They are often equipped with apparatus which enables bags of sorted mail to be dropped at special wayside points while the train is traveling. At the same time other bags can be picked up for sorting on the train during the journey.

Freight Trains

With freight, we come to the reason for the very existence of railroads. We have seen how the earliest railroads were built to haul coal and minerals from the mines and how this material and other heavy freight were the mainspring of railway building in many countries. Freight, rather than passenger traffic, is still the most important reason for the existence of railroads. Consider their ability to haul at considerable speed across country a load equivalent to the cargo of a fair-sized ship, and to do it with a crew sometimes as small as two and never more than a handful.

To gain the full advantages of railways, the load must be at least in the hundreds of tons and be carried considerable distances. Trucks can handle small consignments as well as if not better than trains, and probably more quickly. Where the size of the consignments rises into several tons,

A freight train in America today, with five diesel units at its head. The train is crossing a typical high trestle bridge.

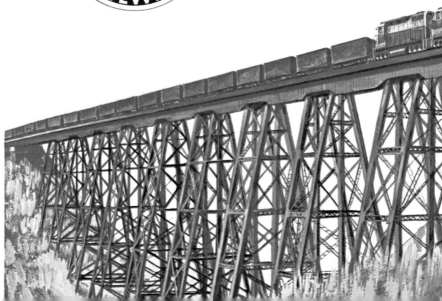

however, the railroads have evolved effective means of handling goods that are proving highly competitive.

The most useful method of door-to-door transport used by the railroads is the 'container'. Basically, this is a box in which consignors can pack all their goods themselves. The box is then carried by truck to a railhead where it is put on a train for the trunk part of its journey. At the end of its rail trip it is put on another truck for delivery. This system has been in use on some railroads for something like forty years, but it is only recently that the merits of the system have been universally recognized and the method widely adopted elsewhere. In addition to special railroad vehicles, there are ships and even airplanes adapted especially for container carrying. The great advantage to the customers is that the goods themselves are never handled or disturbed from door to door. For the railroad, there are advantages in having only one large unit to handle. Containers can be of many sizes and types. Examples are

Piggy-back in the United States: road trailers on flat cars.

refrigerated containers for meat; containers with special fittings to carry glassware, pottery, bicycles; open containers for bricks and roofing tiles; and pressurized containers for powdered materials which can be packed into them or emptied by compressed air.

Sizes are now beginning to be standardized, although many small, sometimes wheeled or collapsible (for returned empty purposes), containers are not covered in this way. The larger containers have an international standard of 8ft. × 8ft. by 10, 20, 27, 30 and even 40ft. in length. Currently in the United States the largest standard size measures 8ft. × 8ft. × 40ft. and holds up to 23 tons of cargo. Such containers can be handled by standard cranes and other equipment and can be packed onto trucks — or ships — as unit loads, the number per vehicle depending on the size.

Similar to the container train is a system used extensively in North America called the piggy-back. Here the 'container' is a complete semi-trailer which forms the rear section of a tractor-trailer unit. The tractor is uncoupled and the complete trailer is loaded onto a flat car. At the other end of the (often very long) trip, the trailer is unloaded, another tractor unit is coupled to it and off it goes to its final destination. Piggy-back volume in the United States is well over one million cars. There are variations of the idea in Europe, the French having produced a particularly successful system in which the trailer wheels are run into special 'pouches' sunk below the floor of a flat car, thus reducing the height of the load. Again for obvious reasons, this has been named the 'Kangarou' system.

In some countries with gauge problems there is a further variant in that railroad cars of one gauge can be mounted on other special rail-fitted cars of a different gauge to cover part of their journey and obviate unloading and reloading their contents.

Another important new idea is that of bulk trains — trains usually with a fixed number of cars, all of the same type, that only rarely have to be uncoupled. They can carry a fixed quantity of, say, coal, iron ore, steel, oil or cement, and their running is worked out to suit a particular industry. They

Merry-go-round non-stop coal
train in Britain.

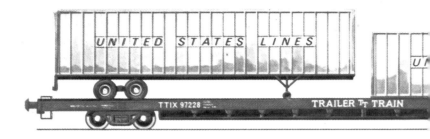

are especially useful where large quantities of raw or semi-processed material have to be transferred regularly from one point to another. A train may run several times a day or only once a week, but because it is known when and where it will run, what the load will be, how much engine power is needed, and so on, it is a very convenient unit for the railroads to handle, and they can reduce their charges to firms using this system. There are many such trains for oil products and there are regular trains carrying nothing but automobiles on special cars.

For bulk coal British Railways have come up with the 'merry-go-round' train. This is a train of large hopper cars semi-permanently coupled together as a unit. They run from coalfields to bulk users, such as large power stations and, when they arrive, run slowly around a loop line without stopping. Apparatus on this loop line causes the bottom doors of the hopper cars to open at the right places and the coal falls into hoppers underneath the rails. The bottom doors are also closed automatically and the train then runs back to the coal mines, where it runs around another loop line. This time, as wagons reach the right spot, overhead hoppers load them with just the right amount of coal. British Railways have estimated that they could move, in these trains, five million tons a year in 205 wagons, instead of the 2,000 which would be needed for conventional working. The principle involved is of economizing by getting good equipment and then using it intensively.

The unit train—a still more refined version of the bulk train —is obviously suitable for coal, ores, petroleum products (in tank cars) and so on, but would not seem to be useful for

U.S. trailer-train car shown loaded with 40 ft. container plus 40 ft. trailer.

goods in smaller quantities. With the container system, however, unit trains can also be used for these, provided there is a sufficiently regular flow of traffic between two points to make the service pay. These trains take the container, not its contents, as the basic load, and the customer pays for the right to use the capacity of a container of one of several sizes. What the customer puts into the container is his business. The trains consist entirely of specially built high-speed flat cars on which containers can be carried. There are special terminals provided with giant straddle cranes which can transfer these containers from road to rail and vice versa very quickly and very gently.

Trackside apparatus reads number and ownership of moving car from colored code.

The containers are distinctive in appearance and specially built of light alloy for the purpose. In the United States, plans are in progress for setting up a network of terminals for container trains. These terminals will be placed at strategic locations around the United States for rapid handling of freight in 27ft. × 40ft. containers. British Railways has placed great hope in its concept of the container train, which they call Freightliner.

A train of these Freightliner cars and containers of various types has toured Europe, and a European Freightliner service is to be set up with the containers carried across the North Sea in specially built ships. Harwich, England is being developed as a container-handling port and similar facilities are now in existence at Zeebrugge, Belgium to form the European end of the ferry service. Other ports are also being fitted for container handling.

In the United States the Reading Railroad has decided that it will offer to send a locomotive and a train crew anywhere on its tracks at any time, given two hours' notice, to haul a ready-loaded train of not more than 20 cars direct to any other point on its system. This service gives the cars a direct run without passing through classification yards, changing engines, or changing crews. In this way the railroad can give at least as good a service as a whole fleet of trucks and often a better, faster one.

The special train has another advantage. In the past it was

sometimes held against railroads that once a car had left a station no one knew where it was until it turned up at its destination. Goods sent by truck, however, were in the personal care of a driver the entire time and if anything went wrong he would telephone his employer. This drawback, very real to traders under pressure from their waiting customers, is being tackled by the railroads in a different way. Cars are being fitted, at a standard height from the rails, with a special coded number plate which can be 'read' by electronic trackside apparatus. The apparatus can read all the numbers as the train goes by and transmit the information to a central point. By having a number of 'readers' the whereabouts of any car can soon be traced from the lists 'printed-out' automatically at the central office. Information from the readers can be flashed simultaneously to other points, such as the next classification yard ahead.

The idea of trains designed for one type of load only — minerals, steel, grain, cement, oil or cars — and even molten metal — has already been mentioned, but on some railroads such trains have grown to astonishing proportions. In West Africa, for example, many lines have been built solely to carry minerals and the trains on these railroads may reach a huge size, because the cheapest way of working them is to run very few, very large ones. No matter what size, they need only one crew, and little signalling equipment is needed

Minerals in Mauretania:
trains of up to 17,000
tons run on this Sahara
ore railroad.

because usually only one train at a time is on the main line. The LAMCO (Liberian-American-Swedish Mineral Company) line in Liberia, for example, has 8,100 ton iron ore trains hauled by three diesel-electric locomotives and the 'Miferma' line in Mauretania is designed for 14,000 ton iron ore trains, also hauled by three locomotives controlled by a single crew.

As well as container-like trailer vehicles which can shed their road wheels for the rail portion of the journey, American and British railroads have experimented with a container-like body fitted with both road and rail axles. These 'Road-railers' have simple equipment, worked by compressed air, which can raise one axle and lower the other as required. The vehicles are light in weight and run as articulated trailers on roads. On rails, the front of each is supported on the one in front of it, the front car of all being supported by a special wagon with conventional railroad coupling at the outer end. As railroad cars, they can run at up to 70 m.p.h. and more. In Europe some countries use special road vehicles fitted with rails on which wagons can be carried through the streets to customers' premises.

Internationally, the scene is one of increasing the speed of

Carrying a railroad tank car on a special road trailer.

freight trains everywhere. The United States has many trains running at an average of more than 50 m.p.h. over long distances. In Europe the picture is the same, helped by the Trans-Europ-Express-Marchandises—the equivalent of the passenger trains described in the previous chapter. This service, introduced to compete with fast services on the highways of Europe, is still expanding, but it has already brought about some spectacular reductions in timings. Goods leaving Alicante in Spain early on a Monday morning can be in Dunkirk on Wednesday morning, having covered 1,270 miles, across frontiers, in fifty-six hours. In Europe, especially, freight traffic is speeded by the number of cars owned by the various railroads that can be used as their own by other railroads. This 'common-user' pool of wagons is paralleled by similar pools of containers and pallets (platforms with or without sides, designed to be lifted by cranes or fork-lift trucks, on which goods can be loaded and firmly held, enabling the pallet load to be treated as a single unit). Container traffic in twelve major European countries is in the hands of an international railroad-owned agency called Intercontainer.

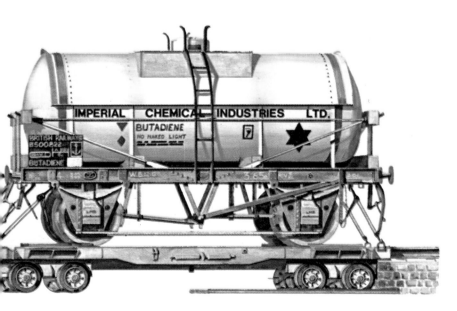

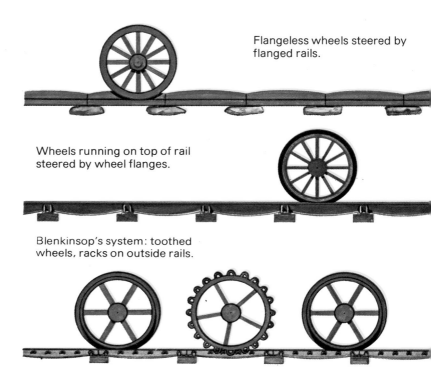

Flangeless wheels steered by flanged rails.

Wheels running on top of rail steered by wheel flanges.

Blenkinsop's system: toothed wheels, racks on outside rails.

Tracks

The first requirement of a train is that it should have a track on which to run, and as far as railroads are concerned the rails are as important as the vehicles which use them; they form the second half of the magic formula: steel wheels on steel rails.

Something of the earlier history of rail development was given in the first chapter. The first effective rails were of cast iron, like those of Jessop, but as soon as traffic on these rails became heavier it was found that cast iron was too brittle and wore too quickly, so the more expensive wrought iron was substituted. This, in turn, became inadequate and eventually, in 1857, the first steel rails were made by R. F. Mushet and laid at Derby, England in a location in which iron rails had worn out in three months. The steel rails lasted sixteen years. Steel gradually replaced iron everywhere, progress being accelerated by the patenting of the Bessemer process of steel-making in 1855 and the subsequent reduction in the price of steel.

Today all rails are of steel. The rails by themselves could not support the weight of the trains and have to have a proper foundation to spread the load evenly over the subsoil.

The exact method of building the foundation differs according to the type of terrain in which it is built, the prevailing weather, the materials available locally, the weight of trains expected, and so on, just as roads differ in their composition. The track foundation not only has to spread the load, but has to be loose enough for the track to drain through it, to hold cross-ties in place and level, and to give a certain springiness to the track.

The foundation materials, or 'ballast', are usually a broken stone such as granite or limestone, but can be slag, gravel, cinders, ash, sand or even hard earth. There is usually a lower layer of large pieces of material, say three to nine inches across, and an upper layer of a half inch to two inches. On this the cross-ties are laid and loose ballast of the smaller size is fitted in between them. The cross-ties, or sleepers as they are called in England, are transverse pieces of wood or other material to which the rails are fastened. They hold the rails in place and at the right distance apart and also play their part in spreading the load. Cross-ties may be of hardwood or softwood, of steel, of pre-stressed or post-stressed concrete, or of concrete blocks under each rail tied together by a metal bar. The choice of cross-ties depends partly on local conditions, for there are some countries where timber cross-ties deteriorate rapidly

Modern high-speed track with
concrete cross-ties and long welded rails.

or are attacked by termites. The number and spacing of the cross-ties depends largely on the weight of trains, but in the United States there are some 3,000 to 3,500 per mile on the most heavily loaded tracks, in France 2,800, and in Great Britain some 2,100.

A type of rail called 'bullhead' was much used in Britain. This has a rail section something like a dumb-bell, with a bulbous head on which the train runs, a thinner, web section below it and another, slightly less bulbous section acting as a foot. These rails

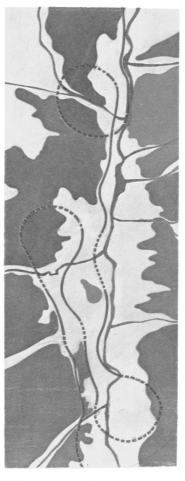

Bridge over the Zambezi Gorge.

Spiral tunnels near Wassen on the St. Gotthard line in Switzerland.

are carried in cast iron 'chairs' shaped to fit them but with room outside the rail to drive in a wooden or spring metal block which holds the rail in place. The chairs are bolted to the cross-ties or fastened down with coach screws.

Bullhead rails are still used, but most countries use a rail that has a bulbous head and a web section, but has a wide foot which can be spiked down directly onto the cross-tie if needed, though generally some form of metal, rubber or plastics baseplate is inserted between rail and cross-tie. These 'flat-bottom' rails are in use now on practically all high-speed tracks. The rails themselves have grown longer and are rarely less than sixty feet long. Most of those on main lines are longer —up to 100 feet or even more. The ends of the rails are joined by 'fishplates', short metal bars placed inside and outside the web of the ends of the rails with bolts passing through the fishplates and rail ends.

Modern practice on fast lines is to weld the rail ends together to make rails of, say, 600 feet in length and then to weld them into even longer lengths after they have been laid. Such rails may be half a mile or even more in length but their elastic fastenings hold them without vibration or slipping under the passage of a train. To take care of expansion of the metal on hot days, the rail joints between lengths of long-welded rail are feathered (i.e., each rail is cut to a fine taper so that the ends can slide alongside each other without disrupting the running surface on which the train wheels run). Long welded track gives very smooth running without the constant beat of the rail joints so noticeable on other types of track.

Rails are laid with a slight inward slope, and the wheels of vehicles are coned to a similar shape when new. On a curve, therefore, as a train is forced outward by centrifugal force the wheels move sideways so that the inner wheels are running on the smallest diameter and the outer wheels on the largest. This changing of wheel diameter helps to steer the train around curves and serves a similar purpose to the differential on an automobile.

A locomotive gives its best performance on the level and loses effect rapidly when it has to climb a gradient. The advantage of the steel wheel on steel rail is quickly lost. For this reason railroads from the earliest days have been laid with gradients as small as possible. A good main line has few gradients of more than 1 in 200 (i.e., a rise of one foot for every 200 feet of distance) though 1 in 100 is acceptable and steeper gradients are not uncommon. One steep gradient, however, can limit the size of trains over the whole line and make it necessary to use locomotives more powerful than would have been needed if it could have been avoided.

In hilly country obstacles cannot be avoided and the railroad must make its own level path. From this need came the embankments and cuttings, the bridges, viaducts, and tunnels which form such prominent features of the railroad landscape. Very steep ascents sometimes need exceptional measures, such as zig-zag lines on the side of a valley up which the train must be alternately pushed and pulled. In a few cases, trains gain

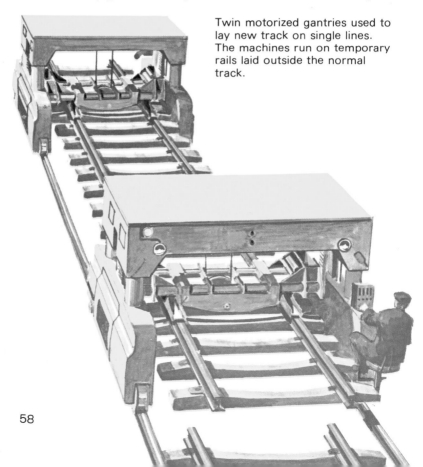

Twin motorized gantries used to lay new track on single lines. The machines run on temporary rails laid outside the normal track.

height by vanishing into a mountainside to appear again above, having executed a spiral turn in a tunnel. Railroads can climb or descend via valleys in the same way, descending against the slope nearly to the bottom, crossing the river on a bridge and then turning to descend again with the valley slope. For still steeper inclines special methods, to be discussed later in this book, are used.

Railroad track is laid today in complete panels (i.e., in lengths of rail to which the cross-ties and baseplates are already attached). The panels are carried on flat cars to the site and placed in position by cranes of many types, sometimes mounted on vehicles especially for tracklaying and sometimes rail or road traveling machines used for other purposes. Where longer, welded rails are to be used, the track is often

Keeping track in good order. This high-capacity tamper packs ballast under and around the cross-ties and lines up the track automatically.

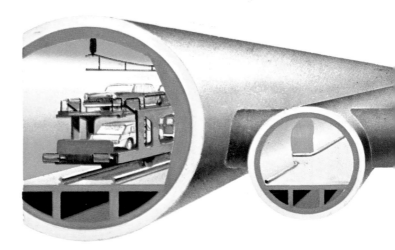

laid with short rails and left until it settles down under traffic. Then the short rails are taken out and the long rails fed over the end of a rail-carrying train into position on the track.

Track maintenance is now highly mechanized, with ingenious machines which can scoop ballast out, clean it, return it to the track and push it under the cross-ties to exactly the right height. The introduction of these machines has revolutionized maintenance work, and fewer men are needed. The men are now organized in large, highly mobile gangs with their own vehicles so that a large force can be used wherever required in conjunction with the machines. With modern apparatus, the work is performed much more quickly than before and the leveling and lining-up of the track can be performed automatically as the machines move along.

Railroad tracks cross frontiers, as we have already seen, but they can also cross the seas. Railroad cars are carried across such stretches of water as the North Sea, the English Channel and the Baltic by train ferries with railroad tracks on their main decks. There are ferries like them along the American Pacific Coast, across European and African lakes, and across wide rivers: they have been aptly named 'floating bridges'. Although the majority of these ships carry freight traffic, passenger coaches, with their occupants, are carried on others. For example, a sleeping car express, with the passengers in

How the English Channel Tunnel might look, with electric trains in two main tunnels and a service tunnel.

A Swiss train ferry, the *Romanshorn,* carrying passenger and freight cars across the Bodensee.

bed, crosses from Britain to the Continent regularly, and passenger trains are carried between Germany and Denmark.

Some wide rivers—like the Severn in Britain—are negotiated by tunnels, and now thought is being given to railroad tunnels under the sea. A four-mile submerged tube is being laid across San Francisco Bay to take the tracks of a rapid transit railroad, and Japanese engineers are investigating the possibility of a twenty-three-mile railroad tunnel between the main islands of Hokkaido and Honshu. It would be known as the Seikan Tunnel and fourteen miles of it would be under the sea.

The long-proposed Channel Tunnel between Britain and France, so often on the brink of being started — and even begun in the 1870's and 1880's — would have at least twenty-one miles under water and be over thirty miles in total length. It would, with a fast electric train service, revolutionize rail communications between Britain and the Continent and be one of the most useful pieces of track ever built.

Railroad tracks, like roads, are expensive to build and to maintain, so no railroad has more of them than is essential. In these days of faster (but often fewer) trains and better signalling it is sometimes found that a railroad has more tracks than it needs. It may be possible to reduce four tracks to three, with the third track signalled for two-way traffic, or even to reduce down to two tracks. Similarly, one two-way track will sometimes perform the work which previously needed two one-way tracks. Good signalling and suitable passing loops are needed in these conditions and the best results are obtained where long stretches of track are under control from one point. Where trains are not too numerous, a hundred or more miles of line may be controlled from one center. This centralized traffic control (C.T.C.) has revolutionized operations in parts of Africa, in North America, and now has a firm hold in Europe and the East. The principle is that from the central point the operator can see on a panel where every train is and the most convenient point for it to pass another train running in the opposite direction, and be able to operate, from a central panel, points and signals which may be controlled 100 miles away. Unless passing loops are very long, it is normally necessary for one of the trains to stop.

Points diverging from the straight can only be taken at low speed, but new types of points, with very long tongues (the flexible sections of rail which move to contact the fixed rails on either side and thus change the direction of the train) enable the curves to be so smooth that the points can be taken at high speed in either direction.

Gentle curves are very important to high-speed train operation, which demands a high standard of track kept in very good condition. Any slight track defect scarcely noticeable in an ordinary train is magnified enormously in high-speed running. Heavy, well-ballasted rails, properly laid and

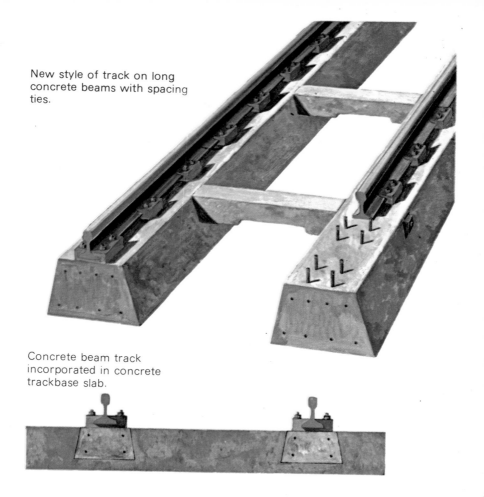

New style of track on long concrete beams with spacing ties.

Concrete beam track incorporated in concrete trackbase slab.

carefully maintained are now thought suitable for speeds of up to 185 m.p.h. or more, but sharp curves would have to be banked with the outer rail high above the inner. As an example, the high-speed New Tokaido Line in Japan has curves with a *minimum* radius of 8,200 feet—more than 1½ miles—and even this needs the outer rail to be nearly eight inches higher than the inner.

New methods of laying track are being tried out, including fastening the rails to longitudinal concrete beams under each rail or to concrete base slabs with various types of flexible pad in between rail and base, but so far the cross-tie-mounted rail still seems superior to all others.

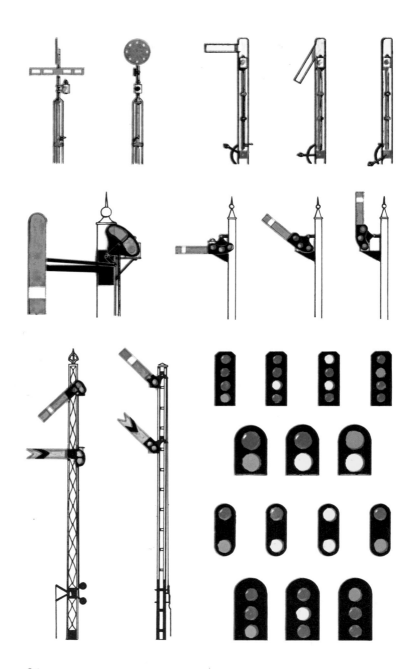

Train Safety

When railroads were young, signalling was not needed. With horses drawing a few cars at walking pace there was no problem. Even with early steam, speeds were low and loads small, and often only one locomotive was running at a time. Signalling is still unnecessary on lines with only 'one engine in steam'.

As speeds rose, the great advantage of railroads—the low friction between rail and wheel—became a disadvantage because trains could not stop quickly, especially when only the locomotive and perhaps one or two manned cars had brakes. The 'brake car' was so called simply because it was fitted with brakes that the guard could apply when the driver whistled for them. Once railroad traffic grew past the point where trains were so few and far apart that they could never come together, something had to be done to tell drivers where other trains were.

From this need came the railroad 'policemen', forerunners of the railroad signalmen, as well as of the police forces employed by railroads all over the world to keep order on their premises and to guard against the pilfering of goods in transit. From the earliest days, the railroads maintained their own police. The stations for these forces also served as 'depots for passengers and goods from or to any of the intervening places'. Hence the railroad 'station'. To show drivers that the line was clear, the policeman assumed 'an erect position with his arm outstretched'. If the line was obstructed he stood 'at-ease'. Some railroads also had signs for 'proceed with caution'. Unless the policeman had a long clear view down the line, the information presented to the driver usually depended on the length of time since the previous train had passed and therefore on the distance it could have been expected to run in that time. A red flag was used to stop the train to pick up passengers

Top row: disc and crossbar signal (1840's) at danger and clear, and slotted semaphore at danger, caution and clear. Middle row: 'somersault' semaphore at clear (1870's) and three-position 'upper quadrant' signal (1910 onward) at danger, caution and clear. Bottom group: a selection of modern semaphore and color-light signals.

New German Railroad centralized signalbox at Osnabrück.

at the police station, so the red light came to mean 'stop' and trains carried a red taillight at night, though this was sometimes turned to blue when a train stopped as a special warning to the train following behind.

While the policeman had to show himself in person, he could attend to only one train at a time, so systems of fixed signals grew up which could be set and left while the policeman attended to another line. Flags or colored boards were generally used by day and lamps by night, with varied colors.

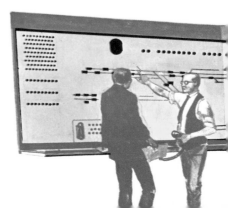

Inside a centralized signalbox controlling many miles of track by signal and points switches mounted on its panel.

One early railroad used white for 'line clear', green for 'caution' and red for 'stop'.

To give trains time to stop, signals were often displayed considerable distances before the danger points they protected. In this way the 'distance'—now 'distant'—signal came into being.

Flags sometimes hung down limply and could not be seen properly, so painted boards were often used. For example, a red-painted board would be turned toward the driver for 'stop' but would be turned on edge when the line was clear. Discs were sometimes used. Boards and discs were often so large, for visibility, that holes had to be cut in them to reduce wind pressure. The railroads were quick to see the possiblities of the early electric telegraph. In the United States the first train dispatched by telegraph was on the Erie Railroad in 1851. As the telegraph came into regular use, railroad lines were split into block sections and the passage of a train from block section to block section was telegraphed ahead from station to station. This system, still the basic method used by railroads, is designed to ensure that only one train is allowed to be in a section at any one time.

Eventually, the idea of working signals from a central point by wires and levers came into being and the signals themselves crystallized into the familiar 'semaphore' arms, named originally after the Navy-type semaphore signalling chains in use at the time. The railroad signals had an arm that signified 'stop' when horizontal and 'caution' when at an angle of 45°. To show 'clear' the arm slotted vertically out of sight into the post. This in turn gave way to arms which meant 'stop' when horizontal and 'clear' when at an angle either up or down.

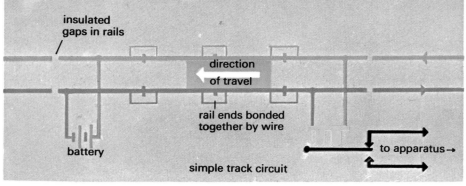

insulated gaps in rails

direction of travel

rail ends bonded together by wire

battery

to apparatus→

simple track circuit

How a track circuit works.

A program machine which operates points and signals automatically from a punched timetable.

The 'caution' aspect was reserved for separate 'distant' signals with different colored arms. At night, the lighting system evolved to green for 'clear', yellow for 'caution', and red for 'stop'. From these have sprung modern color-light signals, visible by day and night for more than half-a-mile. (Over a mile for 'searchlight' type signals.) The busier sections of nearly all railroads now have color-light signals, but many semaphore signals are still in use. The modern section stretches from 'stop' signal to 'stop' signal (as opposed to 'distant' or cautioning signals) including a length of track beyond the signal. This is called the 'overlap'.

Modern signalboxes control all movement on the railroad over a wide area instead of the mile or two dealt with by the older boxes at every station. All signalboxes have the same task, however, whether small or large—to ensure the safe working of all trains under their control and, after that, to ensure that they work in the quickest and best manner appropriate to the class of train. The older signalboxes have a row of big levers needing physical strength to pull down. The levers are connected by wires or rods to the signals and points and are all interlocked so that, for example, it is impossible to set the signals for one route and the points for another. As boxes grew larger and distances longer, power assistance was provided and the levers became smaller, until they were only a few inches long.

Modern signalboxes do not have levers at all, but small buttons, often geographically arranged on a diagram of the tracks they control, which have only to be pushed, pulled or turned to change points or signals operated by electricity or compressed air miles away. Because points and signals often are out of sight of the signalbox, elaborate precautions are taken against the failure of the apparatus and detectors are fitted to signal back to the box that the required change has been made. This is shown to the signalman, usually, by a system of colored lights arranged geographically, like the operating switches, on a diagram. The movement of trains through the controlled area is shown on an illuminated diagram of the track. In later versions, the diagram is sometimes illuminated permanently *except* for the sections occupied by trains. This is a precaution against lamp failure.

The setting up of a route through a complicated network of points and signals in a busy area can take some time, so a system has now been devised under which the signalman has only to push the two buttons at the beginning and end of the route for all points and signals to set themselves automatically. The apparatus is usually capable of 'storing' routes, so that the signalman can set more than one route in advance, the points and signals changing automatically to the next route as the first train clears the sections concerned. The signalman knows which train is coming next because, apart from the time-table, a code describing each train is passed from box to box — sometimes automatically — ahead of it.

On open track, where there are no junctions, trains can safely be left to signal themselves, each train turning the signal behind it to red as it enters the next section. When it reaches the section beyond, the red light, now two sections behind, turns yellow and the next, immediately behind the train, turns red. When the train then enters the next section, the first signal will turn green, so that every train leaves behind it, in order from the train, first a red, then a yellow, and finally a green signal.

All this is achieved, like the lights showing the train position, and nearly everything else in modern signalling, by track circuits. The simple track circuit is the foundation of modern signalling. The principle is that the track is divided into sections with insulation at the ends to separate them. A low-voltage electric current is passed through one rail to the other end of the section and then back along the other rail. When a train enters the section, it breaks the circuit and the current will take the shorter and easier path through its wheels and axles. The change in the track current flow is detected and many kinds of electrical apparatus can be controlled from this initial stage. When the train leaves a section, current flows through the rails again.

The London Underground has ingenious machines which carry the day's timetable, or 'program' punched in code form on a plastic roll. As this roll passes through the machine it sets the points and signals correctly for the next train. When the train has passed, the machine sets the track properly for the next one, and so on.

Signals may indicate the state of the track with the utmost reliability, but this is of little use unless the locomotive crews can see them in all circumstances. To make their task easier, some railroads now have apparatus which shows by colored lights in the cab the same indication as those shown by the normal signals. This is usually done by passing coded impulses through the rails, the frequency of the impulse indicating the state of the line and fixed signals and operating appropriately colored lights on the train—red, yellow or green (double-yellow is sometimes used as an 'advance caution').

Cab signalling in Stockholm. Signals
show as lights on the cab wall.

The extension of this system could well result in the disappearance of trackside signals altogether, for except in emergency they are not needed. On sections with signalling worked by the trains themselves, neither signalmen nor signals would be required.

The method of working long single lines by centralized traffic control (C.T.C.) has been mentioned before. It began in the United States in 1927 and can be as simple as the provision of a telephone at passing loops to let the train crews call in and report their position and ask whether they should wait for a train to pass or continue. Generally, however, there are power-operated points and signals at such loops with the controls concentrated at one or more desks at a central point. The

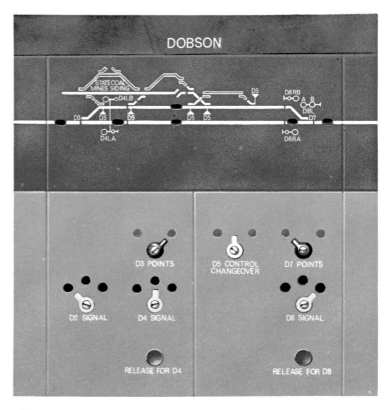

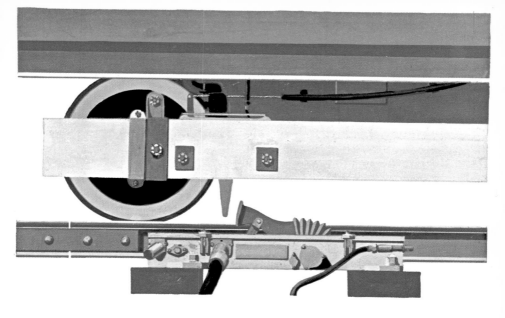

Part of a C.T.C. panel for control of points and signals (*left*).
A subway train stop device (*above*).

controller at this point has a diagram showing him where every train is and can operate the whole stretch — possibly of two or three hundred miles — from his one desk. This saves manpower strung out along the line and also the many telephone conversations needed between distant operators. The one man (or two) at the console desk can see the whole line and control it from one place.

Another safety device is the automatic warning system, which sounds a warning in the cab of a locomotive when a distant signal is passed at 'caution' or a color-light signal at any color except green. If the signal is at 'clear' a bell rings, but if at 'caution' a horn sounds and the driver has three seconds to take full control. If he does not acknowledge the signal in that time by taking control the brakes are automatically applied. A visible indicator in the cab remains as a warning until the next signal is passed at clear.

Finally, some urban lines are fitted with a train-stop device at every 'stop' signal. If a train passes a signal at red a lever beside the track 'trips' a valve on the train and applies the brakes.

Tractive Power

The early development of the steam locomotive played an enormous part in the acceptance of railroads as the dominant means of inland transport in the last century or more. Without it we might not have had our present national networks of railroads at all. Steam was the leading source of power in the nineteenth century for all kinds of industrial activity—steamships, mills of every kind, factories, even for plowing on the larger farms, and the steam railroads fitted logically into the business of industrialization.

Over this long period the powers of the steam locomotive were developed beyond the dreams of the most far-sighted of the pioneering engineers. They became fast—Britain holds the record for speed with 126 m.p.h. by Sir Nigel Gresley's streamlined *Mallard*—and powerful—the United States has 570-ton locomotives capable of hauling 18,000-ton ore trains. A steam locomotive could be built for almost any task. Why then, though continuing to do fine work in many parts of the world, have they vanished from many areas, and why are they on the way out in many others?

The reasons are both economic and social. The diesel and electric locomotives which are taking the place of steam are more costly than their predecessors, but they are available for work over much longer periods. A steam locomotive had to visit a depot for attention every day. When its fire was out, it took a long time to light it and reheat the boiler to raise a working pressure of steam.

This greater availability makes the more expensive equip-

ment cheaper in the end. For example, a diesel switch engine can work twenty-four hours a day for a whole week or more before paying a visit—a short visit—to its depot. Because the diesel or electric locomotives can do more work, fewer of them are needed. Further, they can usually maintain a higher average speed than steam units and can work more trains as a result. In fact, steam locomotives were never very efficient at turning coal into energy—only about seven percent of the available heat was used—and the same coal could be better used in a power station to produce current to drive an electric locomotive. This situation was made worse by a world shortage of the large coal on which locomotives ran best—attributed to mechanical mining methods breaking the coal down more than hand mining. Oil firing has been adopted in some countries to overcome some of these difficulties.

Steam locomotives needed a driver and a fireman, but diesel and electric locomotives need only the driver, although it may be necessary to take a second man on long distance trains. In addition, the necessarily dirty nature of steam locomotive work of all kinds, including maintenance as well as driving, has become less acceptable today.

Electric and steam locomotives existed side by side for a long time, the cost of electrifying lines ensuring that electric trains were confined, generally, to the more important routes. The diesel locomotive, however, could run on the same tracks as the steam locomotive and also observe the same signals. The diesel challenge was more immediate and more urgent than anything which had gone before.

The first diesel locomotive was in service as early as 1894 at

A Garratt-type locomotive with one boiler feeding two engines.

Hull, with an engine designed by W. D. Priestman, and another early designer was Akroyd Stuart, but it was not until Dr. Rudolf Diesel saw the possibilities of the engine which now bears his name, and its railroad potentialities, that the diesel locomotive began to assume importance. Briefly, the diesel engine is a compression-ignition engine: oil fuel is ignited by the heat generated by the compression of air. Because air alone is compressed, instead of a fuel-air mixture as in a gasoline engine, there is no risk of 'backfire' and the compression ratio can be much higher than with, say, a car engine.

The load on a locomotive is much higher than on a road vehicle, so the problem of transmitting the power of the engine to the wheels is more difficult. The engine must run at a fairly

A typical single-cab General Electric diesel-electric locomotive body.

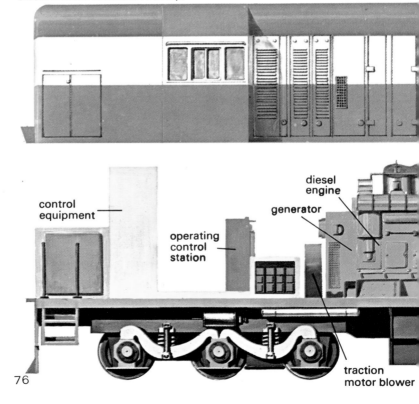

control equipment

operating control station

diesel engine

generator

traction motor blower

high speed to develop full power; it cannot start on full load like a steam engine.

There are three main ways of transmitting the power. For small locomotives and railcars mechanical transmission can be used, much the same as in a truck, with a gearbox to select the appropriate ratio between engine speed and road speed. The main difference is that some form of fluid flywheel or fluid coupling is nearly always used instead of a normal friction clutch, allowing the load to be taken up smoothly.

The main type of drive used on the world's diesel locomotives, however, is less direct but more flexible. The diesel engine has no connection with the wheels but drives a large generator. This in turn drives electric motors which turn the

How the main equipment of a diesel-electric locomotive is arranged (bottom). This versatile type is available for several gauges.

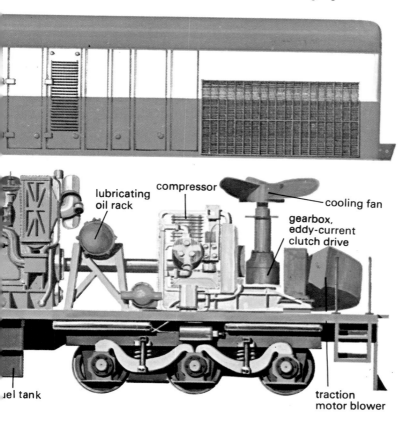

lubricating oil rack

compressor

cooling fan

gearbox, eddy-current clutch drive

traction motor blower

ıel tank

wheels through gearing. The principle is simple and the drive very effective. There is no gearbox to worry about since the electric motor, like the steam engine, adapts itself to the load.

There is another type known as the hydraulic drive, which has been developed mainly in Germany but has been adopted on a fairly wide scale elsewhere. The engine in this case drives a torque converter, which is a hydraulic means of magnifying or reducing the power put into the driven end to give more or less power, at lower or higher speeds, at the other end. The engine drives a type of centrifugal pump, called the 'impeller'. This forces the fluid filling the torque converter casing against the blades of a turbine, causing it to rotate and drive a shaft which, through other shafts and gearing, drives the wheels.

The 'straight' electric locomotive has been with us since

Right: the *Mistral* en route between Paris and Lyons. Below: head-on view of South African electric locomotive with *Blue Train* roundel. Bottom: Swiss electric 'push-pull' train running locomotive first.

1879, when Werner von Siemens's first tiny locomotive ran for four months hauling passengers at the Berlin Trades Exhibition, and there is little doubt that the railroad future lies in electrification.

Electrification, however, is costly because it needs a whole system of electrical substations and cables to bring the power to the track, and the track itself must have, along its whole length, either an overhead supply (catenary) or an extra rail which the trains can continuously tap to pick up power. It can only be used, therefore, for lines carrying heavy traffic. For main line electrification the overhead system is best, but for shorter, urban and suburban services, third, or third and fourth, rail systems have much to commend them. For underground railroads they are almost essential, as they reduce the headroom needed and hence the cost of tunnelling. Power may be supplied as either direct or alternating current ('d.c.' or 'a.c.'). Until recently it was generally thought that d.c. motors were the best for locomotives, and these are still the main type used. The current supplied from power stations is always a.c., which can be transmitted, at high voltage, at a reasonable cost. The first task of a substation is to lower this high voltage to one suitable for transmission over the railroad network. If the railroad uses third rail distribution the substation also has to 'rectify' the supply, turning it into

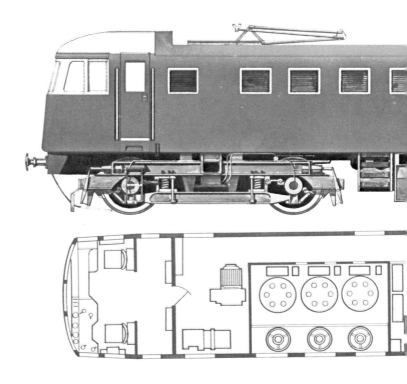

British Railways 3,300-h.p. a.c. electric locomotive. The three rectifiers which convert a.c. to d.c. are on the center line to the left.

direct current at a comparatively low voltage such as 750 V. d.c. Other d.c. systems may use higher voltages, up to about 3,000, but with overhead distribution to the trains. The locomotives can either use this current at the voltage at which it is picked up or step it down before it is fed to the motors.

When alternating current is supplied, as it is in the latest systems, it is distributed by an overhead catenary at a high voltage (e.g., 25,000 V.) and at the normal industrial frequency supplied by the power grid of the country concerned. This high voltage is first transformed to a lower voltage in the locomotive and then either used to feed a.c. motors or rectified for d.c. motors. In the confined space of a locomotive it is

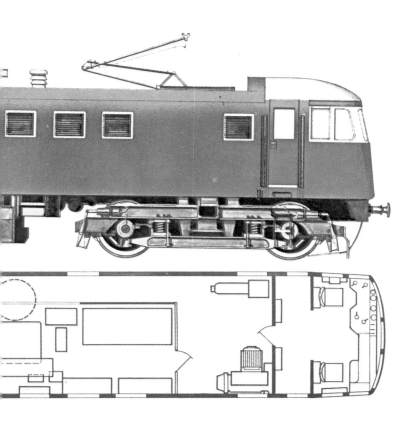

essential that apparatus for rectification be kept small, and great strides have been made with transistor type rectifiers using either silicon or germanium. The use of high-voltage a.c. enables much lighter overhead equipment to be used than is needed for lower-voltage d.c. and also fewer substations are required.

As with diesel-electric locomotives, the final drive in electric locomotives from motors to axles is through a gear train, and the ratio of these gears can be adapted to the work for which the locomotive is intended. Thus one unit could be geared for high speeds with light loads and another unit for heavy loads at low speed.

Electric and diesel-electric locomotives can make use of electrical braking, reducing the wear on the wheels caused by applying the normal brake blocks. In effect, the electric motors are switched to operate 'in reverse' as generators driven by the wheels. In generating current they absorb energy and brake the train. The electrical energy has to be dispersed as heat through banks of resistances (rheostatic braking), but straight electric locomotives can be arranged to feed the power back into the current supply system (regenerative braking).

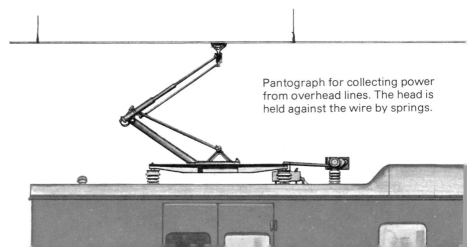

Pantograph for collecting power from overhead lines. The head is held against the wire by springs.

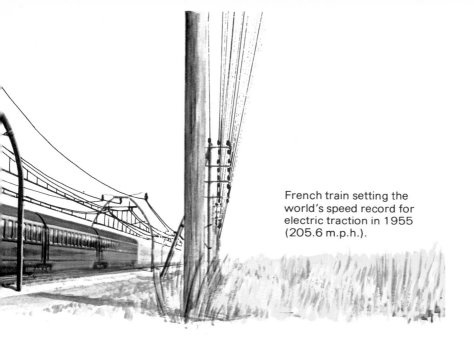

French train setting the world's speed record for electric traction in 1955 (205.6 m.p.h.).

In postwar years the French National Railroads have taken the lead in experiments with industrial frequency electrification, and in tests made in 1954–55 they achieved some remarkable results with special test trains and suitably geared locomotives. Two locomotives, on successive days, hauled the streamlined three-coach test train at 205.6 m.p.h. Spectacular as this effort was, the more mundane tests undertaken to prove the reliability of electric traction were probably more important and far-reaching in persuading other countries to adopt similar electrification schemes. Perhaps the most important point is the enormous power reserve of electric locomotives which, drawing on a central source instead of generating their own current, can give much more than their nominal power for short periods. This enables them to accelerate swiftly and to run at an even, high speed regardless of gradients. Electric locomotives can now be built to run on more than one type of current supply, simplifying the working of through trains over railroads with different systems.

Diesel and electric locomotives can both be worked 'in multiple', which means that two or more locomotives can be coupled together and operated by a single crew. Some

American trains can be seen with five or six diesels at their head, all worked by one crew. As the pull of all these locomotives tends to put a great strain on couplings—and sometimes breaks them—the modern tendency is to put the extra locomotives at various points along the train, controlling them by a radio link from the locomotive at the head of the train. A later development is control by sensitive apparatus on the 'slave' locomotive which detects when the brakes are being applied or when more power is needed by the behavior of the part of the train ahead.

Although we have dealt with locomotives so far, exactly the same types of motive power can be applied to multiple-unit trains (i.e., trains without locomotives but with small, often under-floor, power units distributed among the cars). The lighter diesel railcars usually have mechanical transmission, but the more powerful ones can have either electric or hydraulic transmission. Electrical controls allow gear changing to be carried out simultaneously along the train in the same way as with locomotives running in multiple.

Freight trains are always locomotive hauled, though multiple-unit freight train sets have been mooted before now, but passenger trains can either be multiple unit or locomotive hauled. Which method is used depends largely on whether a train is always to be of the same formation, irrespective of the number of passengers wanting to travel, or whether the addition of extra cars at peak time is necessary. In the latter case, the locomotive is the answer, though it is sometimes possible to add an extra car to a multiple-unit train designed for the purpose. Many people consider that a locomotive-hauled train gives a smoother, quieter ride and is preferable for longer distances. The power cars of some fixed-formation trains are as powerful as many locomotives and can be loaded accordingly, but generally the power of a multiple-unit train is no more than is needed for the service for which it was designed. To make it otherwise would be wasteful.

There *are* electric switching locomotives in some countries such as Switzerland, but generally it is not economic to electrify a switching yard on the overhead system and dangerous to do it by electrified rails when workers have to walk along examining cars and loads. For this reason, switching

European type of diesel switch engine with steps for crew.

is nearly always done by diesel locomotives—either diesel-mechanical for low powers or diesel-electric or diesel-hydraulic for higher ratings. They are usually geared to give a big hauling capacity (a high 'tractive effort') at low speeds, but some of the larger types are arranged to be able to work short trips if required with freight trains or even passenger trains when no heating is required.

Many experiments have been made with gas-turbine locomotives, and there are a number of them in use, but it has been found that such locomotives are not economical unless they can be used in conditions which keep them working at full power. In practice, this means long uninterrupted runs with heavy trains, and such conditions are found in few European countries. In the United States and the Soviet Union there is more scope, and the Union Pacific has some seventy gas-turbine locomotives, mostly 8,000 h.p. units used to haul heavy

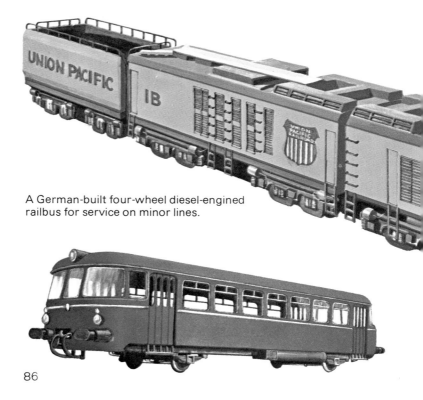

A German-built four-wheel diesel-engined railbus for service on minor lines.

coal trains of up to 5,000 tons on a 500-mile stretch of line with heavy gradients which rises to over 8,000 feet above sea level. This combination of long run, high altitude and heavy load is ideal and the gas-turbines do well here, but they have not been adopted on this scale elsewhere.

A new generation of small gas-turbines based on aircraft types is now appearing on experimental trains. These give such high power for weight—1,100 h.p. from a recent three-ton French unit, for example—that they may have a considerable future. Both Canadian and United States railroads have trains using these new units which are compact enough to go under the floors if required. The French reached 144 m.p.h. in July 1967, with a two-car unit powered by the 1,100 h.p. gas-turbine just mentioned. For high speed work these units could be ideal.

In addition to the multiple-unit trains discussed, there is a future in undeveloped countries and on branch lines elsewhere for light, self-powered diesel vehicles to carry passengers, mails, and freight.

Powerful three-unit gas-turbine locomotive used on heavy coal trains by the Union Pacific Railroad.

Typical
station of a
New York
suburb.

Handling Passengers

Journeys by railroad begin and end at stations and, small or large, they are the railroad's show window and must offer the passenger all he is reasonably likely to need in the way of service. In the country this may be no more than a stopping place alongside the track, in some cases without even a platform or shelter, as long as it is a recognized place for the train to pick up and set down passengers. A large city terminal or through station, on the other hand, must offer many personal services for passengers. Larger stations frequently have railroad-controlled hotels attached to them. A well-equipped station, with its waiting rooms, restaurants and shops, has in fact been called a 'day hotel'.

The main purpose of a railroad station, however, is to provide a place where all the functions required to get a passenger and his luggage into or out of his train can be performed as effectively as possible. The first need of the passenger is to know what trains are available to his destination, how long they take and where, if anywhere, he has to change. This information is all shown on printed timetables and train indicators in any fair-sized station, and if there are any other questions, such as whether a meal can be obtained on the train, there is an information booth to help the traveler. In addition to answering questions, information booths can usually supply, free of charge, printed train schedules for particular routes and free leaflets describing towns and cities of interest.

On most lines the traveler needs no more than his ticket, but if he is traveling by popular train or wants a sleeping berth, he will have made a reservation and booked his ticket in advance. Ticket reservation dates back to the days when particulars of a traveler's journey were actively entered in a

Large through station with many platforms and full passenger facilities. Steam locomotives have now practically disappeared in the United States and many other countries.

book, but today he is given a pre-printed ticket or a ticket printed on the spot by a machine at the ticket window. Such machines are often arranged to make an automatic record of the sale for accounting purposes. Reserved seats are marked off on a train plan, and most large stations in the United States and Europe can reserve seats on trains in many other cities either by telephone or by computerized reservation services which keep a central record of all reservations at a large number of stations and can tell any station which seats—or sleeping berths—are available and on which part of the route.

For many luxury and businessmen's trains, tickets will not be sold unless seats are known to be available. In summer, when many people want to travel on vacation and especially on weekends, seat reservations increase in volume. Again, the number of tickets sold for particular trains sometimes has to be limited, especially where the trains connect with ships of fixed passenger capacity. Sometimes station staff have to be experts at crowd control. Keeping waiting passengers in line

Ticket printing machine.

while their train arrives and is cleared for their journey requires skill and patience.

Even holiday crowds are dwarfed compared to those carried for special sports events. Although not so many in total number, such crowds want to arrive, and still more depart, all at the same time. Stations near sports stadiums are usually specially designed with extra capacity to allow thousands of people to flow smoothly into and out of trains which appear, one behind the other, with clockwork regularity.

Analogous to special services for sports are excursion trains to vacation resorts. These excursion trains have a long history,

Passenger-operated ticket machine selling tickets of various prices.

and were popular as early as 1840. Special rates are offered for travel by one train only, and the routes used are in some cases never employed by ordinary trains. The longer-distance excursion train usually has a snack bar for refreshments and is made up of coaches that would otherwise be idle—a factor which, together with the high percentage of seats usually taken, makes it possible to offer the low fares.

At most big city terminals there is a daily morning inrush of people who work in the cities and a corresponding outrush at night as they go back to their homes in the suburbs. These 'rush' or 'peak' hours are difficult and expensive for railroads to handle, for they use so many trains during the two peak periods that no work can be found for many of them during the rest of the day. (The same 'peak' problem occurs with summer holiday weekends, for which extra cars must be available. Such cars may be needed for only half-a-dozen runs a year.) To meet the peaks, the railroads have to tie up their capital in trains, extra platforms, extra tracks and apparatus, and extra staff, none of which would be needed if the traffic could be spread over a longer period by staggered hours of work for commuters.

With so many passengers traveling regularly, an impossible number of ticket sellers would be needed if everyone had to have a separate ticket for every trip. The familiar answer is the commuter ticket, lasting for a week, a month, three months or longer, with the attraction of a reduction in the cost per day as the period of validity increases. This saves the railroad clerical work and the passenger a great deal of time.

Another method, familiar in many large cities, is to sell frequently used tickets by machine. Such machines can be made to accept a variety of coins and give change as well as a properly printed, valid ticket. These machines can take care of the most frequently demanded tickets, leaving the ticket sellers free to deal with the less common varieties.

Where there are mass movements of passengers, or 'commuters', as daily travelers are usually called today, much attention has to be paid to the design of stations to ensure that passengers can reach trains easily and disperse quickly. The

Railroad excursion poster for England's Great Exhibition of 1851.

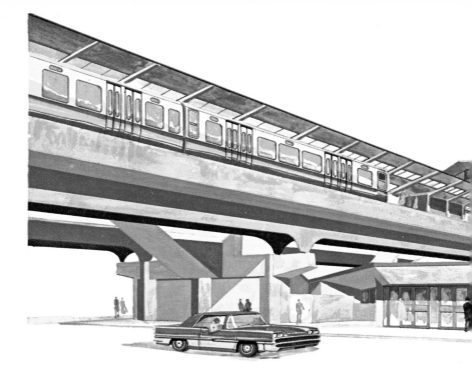

latter is particularly important because passengers arrive to catch trains either individually or in small groups but a train may deposit a thousand or more passengers on the platform within a few seconds. A free flow is essential in order for commuters to get to buses, private cars and subways.

This last need is most easily met, since with an efficient system of underground passages and escalators, streams of people moving in conflicting directions are kept apart. The passengers actually move themselves from one means of transport to the other. Bus lanes, or standing areas where the station is a bus terminal, should be reached by underpass or overpass if there are roads to cross. Some suburban stations will have an official to coordinate bus operation with the arrival of train loads of people, dispatching buses when full and calling up the next scheduled bus or an extra. This method is frequently used when special trains are arriving for sports events.

Other passengers arrive at or leave stations by car. If they

A modern urban station with elevated platforms and ticket office, below. Bus passengers can transfer under cover.

are driving themselves they need parking space where the car can be left in the morning and picked up in the evening. Where railroads have enough land they are providing for this traffic as fast as space can be prepared. Not only does the passenger pay his fare but also a parking fee, so that the operation can help railroads to pay their way. If no parking space is provided the car-owner may decide to drive all the way to work and back and his patronage is lost.

Other passengers are driven to the station by their wives, who then drive home again and have the car for their own use all day. This is known descriptively in the United States as 'kiss-and-ride' traffic as opposed to the owner-driver's 'park-and-ride'. Waiting space is essential near the station entrance where the wives can wait for their husbands in the evening. Also necessary is a through road where they can drop them off and drive away in the morning. This can usually be the same wide road. The same road can also be used for the comparatively small number who arrive and depart by taxicab. At large city terminal stations parking space for private cars is often impossible to provide, so the proportion of people using taxicabs increases and standing space must be found for them.

Apart from passengers making internal journeys, there are many traveling from one country to another and, traditionally, the railroads have always been in the forefront in providing facilities. There is a long history of railroad-owned ports and railroad-owned vessels, on the short sea routes of Europe, the great lakes and rivers of Africa, and elsewhere. At such ports, the railroads provide facilities for passengers to go through customs and passport formalities, and the railroad ships sometimes have a passport office and the officials of one or both countries on board. They also provide offices on board where currency can be exchanged, as well as duty-free shops and bars. The ships themselves are miniature liners with the latest navigational facilities, stabilized, fast and capable of sailing in almost any weather.

U.S. ship loading
containers with mobile
crane—dockside Honolulu, Hawaii.

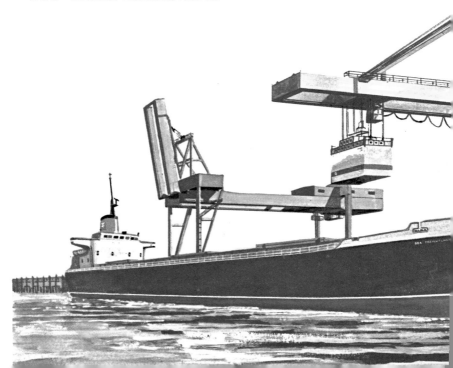

A later development, not yet so widespread, is the serving of airports by railroad. Generally it could be said that at present airports are only likely to be served if they have an existing railroad nearby which is used, or can be used if a short spur line is built toward the airport.

As airports and aircraft grow in size, however, and particularly with the arrival of the 500-or-more-seat 'Jumbo' jets, the picture is changing. There are plans to serve John F. Kennedy International Airport by a subway extension, and an extension of the rapid transit system in Cleveland, Ohio is already serving the airport there. As traffic possibilities increase, the building of a railroad becomes a more attractive proposition both commercially and socially. Paradoxically, however, a swift service to and from a city airport could weaken the competitive value of main line express trains compared with aircraft.

Where no other form of transport is involved and the trains themselves cross borders, it is sometimes necessary for passengers to get off on one side of the border and file through buildings where passports and luggage are checked by the officials of both countries. The train meanwhile crosses the border empty after examination by border officials and waits on the other side for passengers to reboard. On many trains, however, the passengers stay in their seats while officials walk through the train, or the officials travel with the train and perform their work en route.

On international trips of this kind the traveler can avoid frequent inspection of luggage by 'registering' it at the station of departure. It then travels to the passenger's destination without his touching it again, but must be examined by customs officials where he arrives. For internal journeys, luggage can also be carried in the baggage car, but in these days when passengers travel light there is usually room for luggage to travel with the passenger under his own care.

Some of the facilities provided for passengers were mentioned at the beginning of this chapter, but dining service

Services are available to passengers on the platforms during stops.

must be put first. The variety is wide, ranging from excellent, reasonably priced meals in dining cars en route to pre-packaged sandwiches bought on station platforms; from beautifully paneled bars on luxury trains to drink carts pushed along corridors. In Europe, especially, the station restaurant is often one of the best in the town and the favorite eating place of many besides passengers.

Railroads can provide surprising services, once the need is known, such as having hire or rental cars to meet trains — the rental cars can later be left at another station if required — or providing wheelchairs for infirm passengers. Refreshment stands, book stores, flower shops, postal services, telephones and telegraph offices are taken for granted at larger stations, as is the background music played on the public address system between train announcements. Television screens, however, to show how approaching trains are running are still rare enough to provoke comment among even frequent travelers. One day they will be everywhere. Stations will be — as some are now — much more than the starting, stopping and final points of a journey.

Refreshments

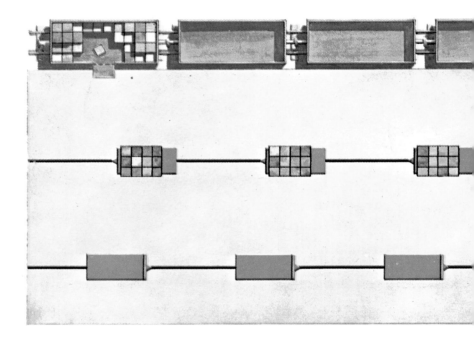

Handling Freight

Unlike the passenger, freight does not often present itself at a railroad depot ready to be put on a train. It is more usual for it to be collected from the sender's premises by a railroad-controlled vehicle, although sometimes the consignor will deliver it to the railroad in his own vehicle. Bulk loads, such as coal or ore, usually start from a complex of sidings privately owned by the mine and end their journey at a similar complex owned by generating station, processing plant, or whatever it may be. This traffic, therefore, is presented as car or train loads and needs no special railroad terminal facilities. All freight, however, has to begin and end its journey at a terminal of some kind and these have to be carefully designed for the type of traffic they are expected to handle.

A small consignment of freight arriving at a railroad freight terminal will normally have been documented on or before collection. If not, this is done when it arrives. In some cases,

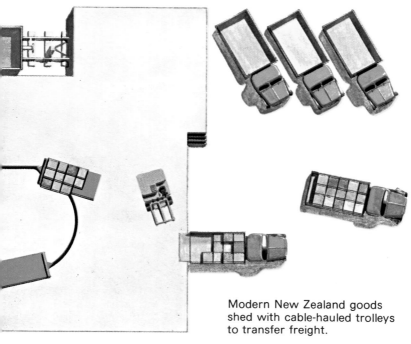

Modern New Zealand goods
shed with cable-hauled trolleys
to transfer freight.

where there is a carload, the freight can be loaded at once
and the car labeled for dispatch on a train going in the right
direction, if not to the nearest terminal. Part carloads are
more difficult and expensive to handle, but it may be possible
to group them with other freight of a suitable type going
to the same destination or in the same direction. If they have
to be carried any distance in the terminal it may be by automatic
trucks steered by a buried cable under the floor or by moving
belts. Ideally, every piece of freight would be put in a direct
through car, but this is impossible in practice.

For the moment, we will assume that we have an individual
car load for which no through train is available. This will
be sent off on a suitable train, with other cars going in the same
general direction, to an intermediate point where there is a
classification yard.

Classification yards are among the biggest and most elaborate of railroad installations as well as the most highly mechanized. They are also among the most expensive, and the
object of most railroads is to have as few as possible, sending

freight by through trains wherever they can. No matter how efficient the yard, freight is not moving while it is in the yard area: it is being delayed.

The object of the classification yard is to collect cars that have come from various directions and make them up into trains for their destinations. If this is not possible because there is not enough traffic for that destination, cars are forwarded to another classification yard nearer the destination.

The procedure is for the freight trains to arrive in the reception sidings at the yards where the locomotive is taken off and freed for other duties. The yard controllers want to know how the train is to be split up and to do that they must know the destination of each car. The make-up of the train may have been sent ahead by telegraph, as is common in North America. If so, the way in which the train is to be split up will already have been decided and it is only necessary to check that the train conforms with the message already received. This can be done by someone walking the length of the train checking the list, but is often done by reading the car numbers over closed-circuit television as the train moves slowly past a camera. If the make-up of the train is not known it is usual for someone to walk down the train reading the destinations and numbers into a walkie-talkie radio or, sometimes, a tape recorder. From these lists the yard controllers work out where the cars must be uncoupled—the 'cuts'—and to which of perhaps fifty or more sidings they must go. The 'cuts' may consist of one car or several together for the same destination.

The train is then pushed slowly by a radio-equipped—sometimes even radio-controlled—switching locomotive—normally a diesel—up a slope leading to a peak called the 'hump'. On the other side the tracks drop away steeply. As the first cut comes to the crest of the hump and goes over, it gathers speed rapidly and moves away from the rest of the train. It is then directed through a maze of power-operated points, beginning with the line dividing into two (the 'king' points) then each line into two again (the 'queen' points), and each of those into two again (the 'jack' points) and so on as required to make up the number of sidings. Before the first

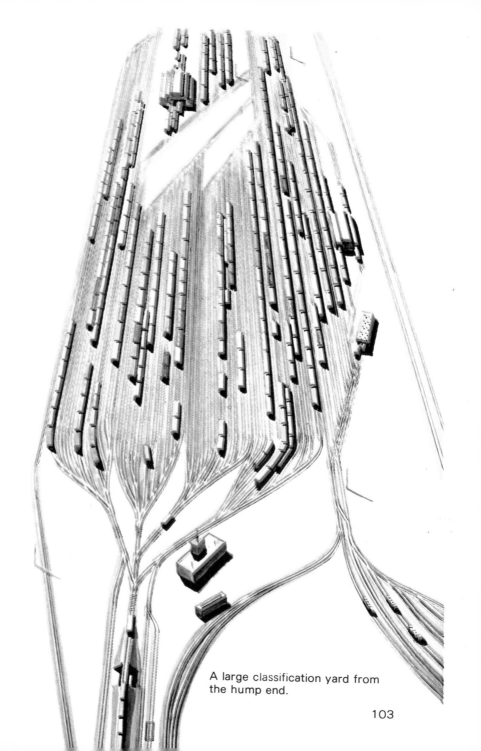

A large classification yard from
the hump end.

cut has gone very far, the second is gathering speed and the points change quickly to divert it to the proper siding. This process goes on until the whole train has been split up and the cars are on the proper sidings.

It will be seen that the working of the points has to be quickly carried out, and this is often done mechanically or electronically. The 'cut' list is made up from the list of car destinations being fed into a unit which makes the point changes automatically, changing points for the next 'cut' as soon as the preceeding one is clear. Sometimes it is done by an operator from the same type of list, using push-button controls which can usually 'store' several cuts so that the operator can work ahead of the cut coming over the hump.

With many tracks, a yard can cover a wide area—the one at Montreal, for example, has 124 sorting sidings or 'classification tracks' and can hold 11,000 cars on its 165 miles of rails. The distance a car has to run under gravity when it is pushed over the hump can vary a great deal, especially as some tracks may be empty and others nearly full. In many yards, therefore, the speed at which the cut must run is calculated by a computer. It is fed automatically with information on the destination siding, the number of cars in that siding, the curvature of the track on the route to be followed, the wind direction and pressure, and the 'rollability' of each cut (i.e., the speed at which it will roll), which depends on the condition of the cars, the number of them, the amount of load in them and other factors. This is measured by radar as the cut rolls down the hump. The speed is then controlled by 'retarders', which press against the wheels and slow the cars down. There are usually two sets of retarders, primary and secondary, and the pressure of both can be varied in several degrees. Recently small hydraulic piston-type retarders

Loading piggy-back road trailers by mobile portal crane.

spread along the sidings have come into use. These have the advantage of being able to give a push to a slow-moving car, as well as being able to slow down a car that is moving too fast. From the sorting sidings, cars are hauled away to form new trains and despatched to their destinations.

Containers, described in some detail in an earlier chapter, can be handled at ordinary freight terminals by mobile cranes or large fork lift trucks, the only essentials being that there should be a suitable siding with road access and room for the crane to maneuver. For full efficiency, however, it is necessary to have special terminals.

'Kangarou' trailers being loaded by tractor on to special pouched cars.

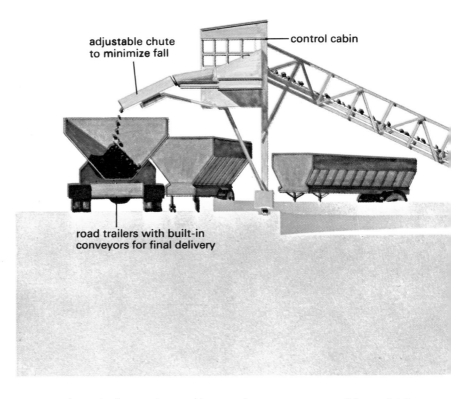

adjustable chute
to minimize fall

control cabin

road trailers with built-in
conveyors for final delivery

A typical container train may have as many as fifteen high-speed cars, each over 60 feet long and able to carry various combinations of containers up to nearly that length. Such a train can carry almost 700 tons of freight in containers and it always travels direct from terminal to terminal, a notice of its load being sent ahead.

A typical terminal may have three sidings each long enough for a whole train (i.e., something over 1,000 feet long). There will also be a heavy-duty road parallel with or between the sidings. Sidings and roadway are spanned by giant cranes able to lift the heaviest container. They are mounted on rails and able to move the full length of the sidings. Such cranes as these can make the transfer between road and rail vehicle in less than two minutes. Two of them can transfer the load of a whole container train to trucks within two hours, freeing the train for reloading in the same time and enabling the best use possible to be made of the special vehicles.

Bulk coal collection and delivery
service to coal dealers cuts
costs and eases handling.

rail car with bottom door

conveyor arm swings
through part of a circle

vibrator and hopper
to minimize
falling distance

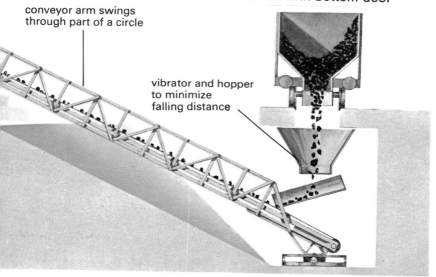

The cranes are fitted with equipment enabling them to handle any of the wide range of containers used or being developed for these trains, and notice of the load received in advance enables the right road vehicles to be ready at the proper time.

Elsewhere, 'piggy-back' vehicles are handled in much the same way, but there is an ingenious 'Flexi-Van', introduced by the New York Central and now spreading to Europe, which is rather different. This is, in effect, a container mounted on a two-axle road bogie to make it into a trailer. When it arrives at the rail terminal, the road tractor backs the trailer, at right angles, against a special rail car and the body then slides off the bogie on to a turntable in the car. Once the body is on the car, the turntable enables one man to turn it parallel with the car for its rail journey.

Tractor trailers are backed over a dock or up a special ramp onto the end of a train of flat cars, the gaps between car

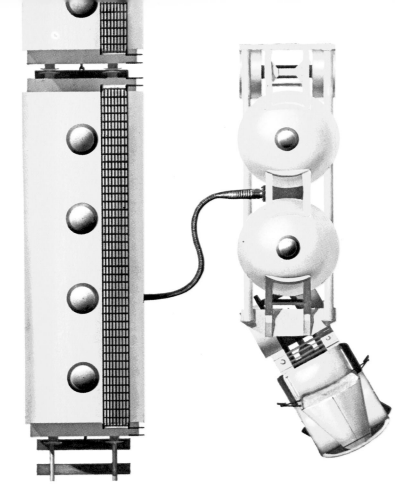

Transferring cement in bulk from rail tanker to road vehicle by air pressure. Below: "Tater-Frater," experimental mechanical refrigerator car with built-in conveyor.

ends being bridged by metal plates. Once the trailer is fastened securely the tractor can drive off to get another trailer. With the French 'Kangarou' and other low-height systems, the trailer wheels are loaded onto the car by a tractor and guided into special slots below the level of the car frame.

The handling of some bulk freight has already been mentioned, but there are other materials which also need special terminals, such as gasoline, oil and lubricants, which need storage tanks, pipelines and pumps to deliver oil into railway tank cars or pump it out. Milk in bulk needs something very similar. Bulk grain and cement and powders need silos and ducts, and the powders often a compressed air supply to load and unload their special cars and containers. Refrigerated traffic may need a special cold storage terminal, or power or fueling facilities to keep refrigerating equipment at work while the car is standing.

One of the problems in countries using domestic solid fuels is to distribute the coal, coke and so on economically to small dealers or fairly small-scale users. An ingenious answer is the centralized coal distribution terminal, which takes block trains of hopper cars direct from a mine and unloads them into a shallow hopper below the tracks feeding a belt system capable of being rotated through a quarter-circle. The belt passes along a jib-type arm, raising the coal to a height sufficient to serve a delivery chute suspended above a waiting truck. The trucks are thirteen-ton capacity hopper semi-trailers which can be hauled to the final delivery point where, using built-in conveyors of their own, they can stack the coal where it is required. A terminal such as this one eliminates the need for small railroad-served coal yards over a wide area and makes possible a more intensive use of cars.

The hopper car used in coal trains is itself a specialized vehicle, as is the refrigerated car, but there are many other examples. Although the car came before the container, in many ways the specialized car now takes over from the specialized container when the flow of traffic grows large enough to warrant it. To take another type of bulk load, for example—automobiles from the factory: special double-deck (and even triple-deck in the United States) vehicles are used everywhere to deliver new automobiles to large distributors. Each of the special cars takes anywhere from six to twelve or more automobiles and a train of these car transporters is an impressive sight. There are other cars with opening roofs and opening sides designed to allow mechanical loading from above or fork-lift loading from the sides. Large light alloy cars carry huge loads of alumina—one type of fifteen-ton wagon in France can carry sixty-five tons of this oxide. These are long low cars, sometimes with a well in the middle between the bogies, for heavy loads; special cars which open in the center or have roll-back roofs for various loads, sometimes fitted or compartmented to take, say, coiled tinplate. All these and many more have their place, but all demand terminals adapted for their needs with the right equipment to deal with them. A hopper car with bottom doors which will release the load in seconds is useless without a special storage hopper beneath the track to receive that load. There is, however, a car used in Germany that is capable of tipping from one

Special car with opening top
for carrying heavy coils of steel
plate safe from the weather.

end or to either side, thus simplifying the whole problem.

Most freight (apart from private siding traffic) must begin and finish its journey by road. Since the most difficult part of the operation is loading, unloading, and transferring goods, it does not matter a great deal if the goods spend another half-hour on the road vehicle if it speeds up the overall time of transit. The tendency is therefore to have fewer and fewer terminals, but to equip those terminals with every modern freight-handling device. When the number is reduced drastically, as it has been in some countries, the number of trains that can be sent directly from terminal to terminal without passing through a classification yard is greatly increased. Accordingly the time of the journey is reduced by hours—or even days. As with the coal distribution terminal, each freight terminal is equipped with road vehicles that range over a wide area. In this way the railroads can provide a much better and quicker service than if the rails served every town individually.

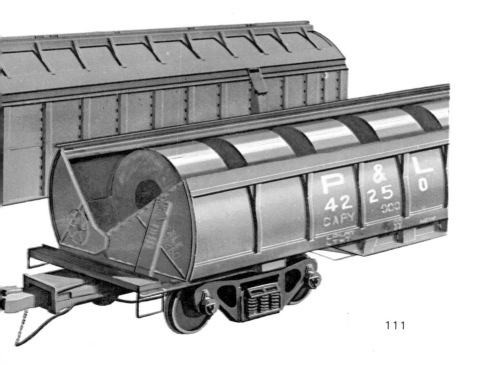

Trains for Cities

The world's first city underground railroad was opened in London in 1863 mainly because of the traffic congestion in the city's streets. Today traffic congestion is still the mainspring of many new schemes for urban, underground or rapid transit railroads.

The first 3¾-mile London rapid transit railroad, the Metropolitan, was worked by steam trains, and a grimy, sulphurous business it must have been. It was, however, quick and, as far as its cars were concerned, comfortable. Londoners flocked to it, over 26,000 passengers a day using it in the first month of its existence. It was not until 1890 that the deep, shield-driven, electrically operated 'tube' railroad came to London

London Underground train in
the days of steam.

Electric locomotive used on the
London Tube railroad in the 1890's.

with tiny four-wheeled 100 h.p. electric locomotives drawing almost windowless cars.

The advantages of railways through city centers were not lost on other cities. Glasgow opened a cable-hauled subway in 1896, Paris its first Metro in 1900, Berlin its 'Kellerbahn' (cellar railroad) in 1902, New York in 1904, Hamburg in 1912, Madrid in 1919, Tokyo in 1927, Moscow in 1935, Stockholm in 1950, Toronto in 1954, Rome in 1955, Leningrad in 1955, Kiev in 1960, Milan in 1964, Rotterdam in 1968, and so on—there are many others. This miscellany of geography and dates shows that the virtues of rapid transit are and have been recognized all over the world for at least sixty years.

The London Metropolitan Railroad was built largely by a process of opening up a huge trench and then roofing it in. It is comparatively simple to do if one can uproot whatever there may be above for a considerable period. The resulting lines are shallow—just below the surface—and easily and quickly reached by short staircases.

In 1904, when subway construction began in New York

City, surface traffic and business congestion were as great as they were in London. Unlike the soft blue clay on which London rests, however, New York's varied topography, much of it solid rock, presented many problems, compounded by the peculiar shape of the city itself. It was fortunate, therefore, that subway construction was started somewhat later on, taking advantage of the newer techniques, as well as the bitter experience gained in other places.

Largely because of the spread of the automobile, rapid transit in the 1960's is enjoying a remarkable world-wide

Subway tunneling at
116 Street and Broadway,
New York City.

boom which is at its height in the United States, the home of the automobile. This is because planners, administrators and engineers realized that their cities would gradually become concrete deserts if enough roads were to be built to take the ever-increasing flood of cars. Their warnings were taken up by city after city, and in 1964 President Lyndon B. Johnson signed an important measure, the Urban Mass Transportation Act. This act authorized Federal grants of two-thirds of the cost of approved transit improvements, provided that, among other things, the proposals were part of a comprehensive scheme

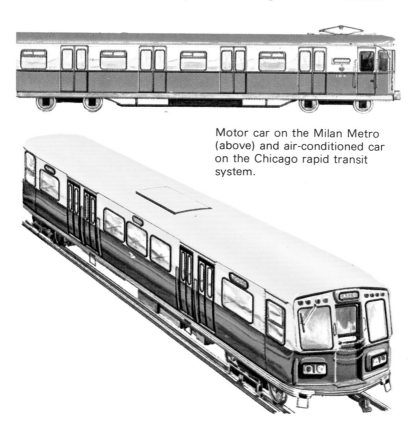

Motor car on the Milan Metro (above) and air-conditioned car on the Chicago rapid transit system.

for the redevelopment and transportation of a complete area.

The promise of federal funds on this scale opened the flood-gates, and nearly every large city in the United States is now improving its rapid transit facilities or is planning to build systems. Networks already exist in New York, Chicago, Philadelphia, Boston and Cleveland. Among the cities planning new systems are Washington and San Francisco.

San Francisco is especially important because its Bay Area Rapid Transit District started from scratch, refusing to take anything for granted. It carried out substantial studies and tests of almost everything concerned with rapid transit. The conclusion they reached was that an electric railroad, with steel wheels on steel rails, was better for their 75-mile rapid transit system than rubber-tired trains or monorails. Their system will also include automatically operated trains, automatic fare collection, and many other advanced features.

Part of the San Francisco line will run in the dividing strip

New York PATH
aluminum transit car

Train on the Lisbon Metropolitano railroad.

between a dual highway, a promising practice already followed by some sections of the Chicago system. When highways and railroads are built together in the same operation there are advantages to both.

To woo the commuter away from his automobile, the rapid transit planners are designing high-speed vehicles which will have comfort almost unknown for this type of travel, with carpeted floors, luxury seating and air conditioning.

Overall planning for transit is usually in the hands of a rapid transit district or a metropolitan transit authority, many of which have been created recently. In some cases they also control the suburban services of the main-line railroads. Some of the new lines are being planned to be partly in tunnel, partly on the surface and partly on 'aerial structures'. In San Francisco, for example, the BARTD scheme will have twenty miles in tunnels of various sorts — including a four-mile sunken tube across San Francisco Bay — and thirty-one miles on aerial structures, the remaining twenty-four miles being on the surface. Even the London Underground, with its shallow covered ways and deep tubes, is not what its name implies, for

Rubber-tired train with guide
wheels on the Montreal Metro.

it has only a third or so of its system under the ground.

In Europe, rapid transit railroads have usually—though not always—had the support of the government, so activity has not been suddenly re-born as in the United States but has been a steady progress interrupted mainly by the two world wars. In London, the Victoria Line has new, quicker routes across the center of the city and is being extended southward. In Paris, a new deep-level double-track tube for main-line size trains is being built to run east and west below the city, with interchange stations for the Metro and connections with the French main-line railroads at each end. The West Berlin underground is extending its lines; Rotterdam has just opened its first rapid transit line, partly in tunnel, partly on a bridge across the Nieuwe Maas and partly elevated; Munich is building its first underground line for the Olympics of 1972; Budapest has a new deep line which should be in service by 1970. Prague and Warsaw have plans, as has Vienna, which already has a light underground railroad—the Stadtbahn. Germany also has a number of sub-surface lines under construction which are designed to take underground trains eventually but will be worked by streetcars, or trains of streetcars, until traffic grows enough to justify full-size rapid transit trains. There are similar lines in Belgium.

In Russia, Moscow and Leningrad are extending their systems steadily and there are new lines in Kiev, Tbilisi and Baku: Kharkov and Tashkent may have their own lines very soon.

Rome has a small modern system that it is expanding, and Milan has a very sophisticated first line which is to be followed by several others. Lisbon, Madrid—unique in having four peak hours a day because so many people go home for lunch—and Barcelona, all have their own lines and all are anxious to expand them. In the north, Oslo and Stockholm have rapid transit lines, and Helsinki bids soon to join them. In South America, Buenos Aires has long had an efficient and busy system. In Japan, Tokyo has a rapidly expanding network, as has Osaka, the second largest city: Nagoya also has a small but swiftly growing system. Places which may soon take their first steps to becoming rapid-transit cities include Lyons, Melbourne, Sydney, Auckland, Wellington, Johannesburg, Bombay, Calcutta, Delhi, Hong-Kong, Cairo, Teheran, Istanbul, Tel-Aviv, Sao Paulo, Lima, Caracas, Kobe and Manchester. Mexico City is just building a first line.

Track for rubber-tired trains. The steel wheels come into use at junctions.

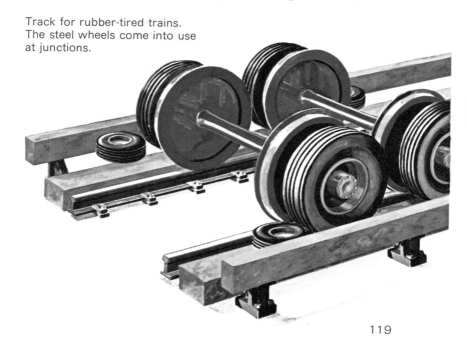

The rubber-tired trains mentioned several times already were first used on the Paris Metro, where three lines are equipped with them. The rubber-tired wheels of the cars run on concrete tracks, and they are steered by horizontal wheels pressing against side guides in the tunnels. Should a tire burst, the bogie sinks slightly and allows normal railroad wheels, attached to the same axles as the rubber-tired ones, to drop down on to conventional rails laid alongside the concrete strips. At points and crossings the strips sink away, leaving the train to negotiate the points on railroad wheels like a normal train. Because the lines take so long to convert to this complicated track, the Paris Metro has reverted to steel wheels on steel rails for its latest stock. Apart from Paris, rubber-tired trains of this type run in Montreal and on the Haifa underground funicular railroad. They will also be used on the new line in Mexico City.

Rapid transit railroads are always seeking to reduce recurring costs, such as heavy bills for labor, so they are in the forefront of experiments in automation. Automatic fare collection is one of the main subjects for experiment at present,

Station on the new San Francisco system, with automatic fare collection gates and air-conditioned train.

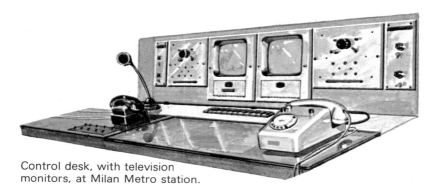

Control desk, with television monitors, at Milan Metro station.

and trials are going on in the United States, Japan, Britain and Europe. If there is a single flat fare a coin can be dropped into a machine to open a turnstile to the platform and no more is needed. Where fares vary with distance the needs are more complicated. The passenger can buy his ticket from a clerk or from a machine, which may also give change. Now there are also machines which will give a whole range of tickets and change, as well as machines to change notes for coins of convenient value.

In the latest systems, the ticket is coded by punched holes or by imposing on it a magnetic pattern, and forms a key to

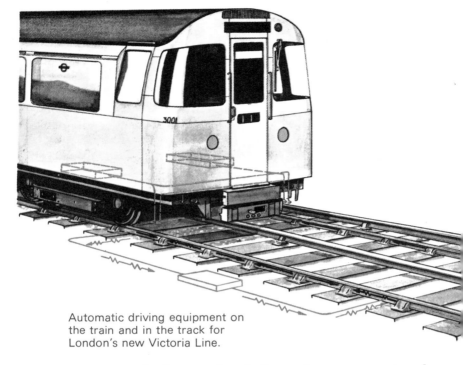

Automatic driving equipment on
the train and in the track for
London's new Victoria Line.

open a gate leading to the platform, the gate returning the ticket as the passenger passes through. At the end of his journey a similar gate, linked usually to a small local or large central computer, 'reads' the ticket and decides whether the right fare has been paid, whether the ticket has the proper date or, for a season ticket, whether it is valid at that station and is still current. This entails the gate searching through its electronic memory for the fares from, sometimes, a couple of hundred stations. An ordinary ticket is retained by the gate at the destination station, but a season is returned. An incorrect ticket will not open the gates and the passenger must go to the station staff. The San Francisco system and London's Victoria Line will be among the first to have automatic fare collection with fares related to distance.

The station staff may consist of one man, as in Milan, where there is a flat-fare system. He sits in a booth and examines season tickets. He also watches the platforms through closed-circuit television, makes loud-speaker announcements and watches that all is well. In an emergency, he can cut off the current from the tracks.

In New York, Paris, London, Berlin, Moscow, Leningrad, Hamburg, Barcelona, Stockholm and elsewhere great strides have been made with automatic train operation, in which trains either pick up commands by induction from trackside cables or the track itself, or have a 'program' on board designed to cause them to run under power, coast or brake according to the characteristics of the journey between any two stations. There are also safeguards against the presence of a train ahead. Paris has one line under automatic operation, as has Barcelona. London has a five-station line working automatically. Another method, adopted in San Francisco, is to bring all trains under the control of a central computer. So far, automatically driven trains all carry a train operator who starts the train and can take over in emergency.

Automatic driving system as tested in New York.

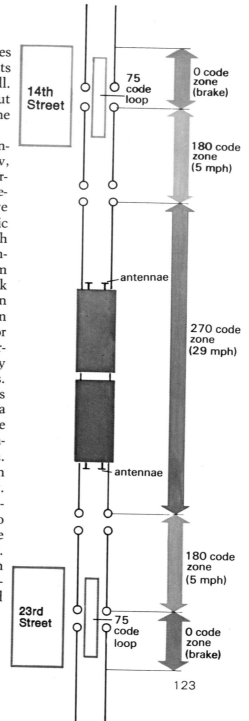

123

The Rail Way Ahead

What is to be the role of the railroad in the future? Is it to remain one of the world's primary means of transport? If so, what will it be like and what traffic will it carry?

The railroad is likely to remain as a vital highway for many years. Recent detailed appraisals have shown that steel wheels on steel rails are capable of much more than was at one time thought possible. Only a few years ago 125 m.p.h. was regarded as the upper limit of speed on conventional track, but 150–160 m.p.h. has now been shown to be possible in regular service provided that the track is carefully laid—in particular, carefully leveled—and well maintained. This means that the 'competition distance' between railroads and aircraft can be lengthened considerably, especially if it is a good many years before VTOL (vertical take-off and landing) aircraft can land nearer city centers and the city-airport journey remains relatively slow.

Canadian National Railroads'
revolutionary new Turbo-Train
for fast services.

Passenger comfort will need special attention if the high-speed trains are to keep their clientele. Ordinary luxury-hotel comforts of seating, food, air-conditioning and a general high standard of train appointments can be taken for granted, but there will have to be a considerable rebuilding and easing of curves on high-speed lines to protect passengers from the effects of centrifugal force. There is a limit to what can be done by 'superelevation' (i.e., raising the outer rail to bank the train as it goes around curves). The train may have to stop on those curves or go around them slowly at times. There is a possibility that new types of suspension that will allow the body of the

124

carriage to move independently of the frame may relieve some of these effects, but they have yet to be tried on a wide scale. It may be necessary to rebuild main lines to reach the proper standards. Even the superb standards of the new Tokaido Line in Japan with 8,200 foot radius curves are not thought good enough, and its extension is being built to yet higher standards. It is a measure of the Japanese faith in high-speed railroads in their crowded islands that it is being built at all, but it is being vindicated by government-assisted work in the United States. The electric-powered Metroliner, operating between New York and Washington, has completed well over one million high-speed car miles, with 76 percent utilization of available seat miles. Another consideration to be watched is the sudden and disconcerting rise of air pressure as a high-speed train enters a tunnel. Only a sealed train can eliminate this, but it might be possible to close all vents automatically at the tunnel approach.

As train speeds rise so does the power needed to operate them. Careful attention will have to be paid to the aerody-

namic shape of the front end of trains, to a generally smooth surface without breaks, and to light but strong methods of construction. These can bring the requirements down to reasonable levels which can be supplied by electric or diesel power. Though the new small gas turbines offer considerable promise, it is probable that the new railroads will be electrically powered with motors spread out along the train. This is because electricity can be generated from several types of fuel or water power, and also because electric motors are capable of giving out much more than their rated power for short periods — valuable in initial acceleration. Electric motors also enable rheostatic or regenerative braking to be used in a speed range where present braking methods, except disc brakes, are likely to fail from overheating.

The new electric railroads already exist in the 320-mile New Tokaido line in Japan and its forthcoming 100-mile extension, in the British London—Liverpool—Manchester line and in the considerably improved New York—Washington tracks picked as the high-speed test grounds of the government-backed electrical trial services.

The new turbines are not so advanced. At this writing the Canadian National Turbo-Trains were still running trials but were expected to start carrying passengers very shortly. The French have had a successful lightweight prototype turbo-train in service, adapted from a standard railcar set, and the British have their 'Advanced Passenger Train' well into the design stage. It is expected to reduce the weight per passenger to only 40 percent of that of a conventional train and to be capable of 150 m.p.h. Even more important than the top speed is the expected very rapid acceleration and deceleration possible with this train. A hydraulic system will control banking on curves to enable them to be taken faster, and newly developed running gear gives a steering action which will take the train through curves without the wheel flanges grinding on the rails and causing wear and tear. The deceleration is obtained from a new form of hydraulic braking which will be so effective that in many cases new signalling will not be needed, since the train wil be able to stop within the limits now allowed. Whether this high rate of deceleration will be within the limits of reasonable passenger toleration remains to be seen. It is not difficult with conventional methods to stop a train abruptly, but not without flinging passengers about.

A smooth deceleration may be achieved by a newly designed British train that relies on aircraft techniques for both bodies and engines. If it is adopted orders for it could well go to aircraft manufacturers already familiar with these techniques instead of the traditional railroad rolling stock builders. The train is expected to be in service by 1973. Some form of automatic control seems essential at these speeds, and no doubt

United Aircraft turbo train.

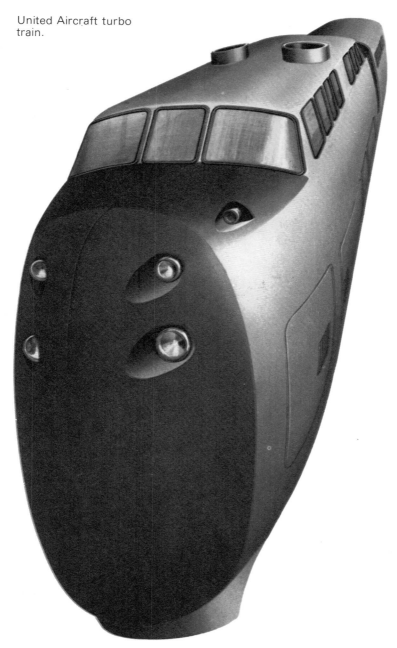

some special devices—perhaps new, perhaps versions of equipment already in use or under trial—could fit the circumstances.

As far as freight is concerned, speed will not need—at least at first—to be quite as high and locomotives will probably be the best form of power. However, permanent-set trains of the container type could well be multiple-units with dispersed motors. The aim will certainly be to run freight trains direct from terminal to terminal at the highest speed possible. The closer this speed approaches that of the passenger trains the better, for the new, expensive railroad tracks will need to be intensively used if they are to be economical. The closer to a uniform speed the trains get, the more can run over one pair of rails. The faster the speed of all types of trains, the more journeys each train can make. In this way fewer trains can do more work and reduce capital costs.

When the New Tokaido Line was built, it was fully intended that it should be used for freight as well as passenger trains, with the freight trains taking only 5½ hours to run between Tokyo and Osaka. Goods would have been loaded in containers and carried on specially-built multiple-unit trains designed to carry containers and including most of the features of the passenger stock. The maximum speed would have been 81 m.p.h. against the 125 m.p.h. intended at that time for passenger trains on the same line.

In fact, the freight trains have never been built, so we have been denied the experience of operating super-fast trains for goods alone, but there is little doubt that this is the direction in which things are moving. If not the New Tokaido, some other line will eventually be moving freight at up to 100 m.p.h.

At high speeds, human reactions become too slow to be entirely trusted unless all operators have the same physical standards as racing drivers or airline pilots. This means, in effect, that the trains will have to have automatic safeguards built into them. At anything over 130–150 m.p.h. they ought to be automatically controlled. Fortunately, the railroad lends itself ideally to automation. It runs on a fixed, predictable track of steel, a material through which electric currents can flow or in which they can be induced. Already speed controls can be imposed on trains from central supervision rooms and systems of full automatic driving have been developed for rapid transit trains which could readily be adapted for main-line use. The uniform running characteristics that such a system imposes will help to make the greatest possible use of the lines—making two tracks, perhaps, do the work done by four today.

To take account of the variations of traffic inevitable when freight and passenger trains are run on the same lines, it is probable that a central computer will be used to watch the running of trains on the whole line. Its commands will replace those given automatically to the train by the signalling

U.S. container train

system—which will be controlled by the train ahead—and act over any driving commands given from the trackside or by a train-borne operating 'program'. An automatic, track-guided radar system will warn trains of obstruction on the line from non-railroad causes (e.g., a stalled road vehicle on the tracks).

In this way the railroads are slowly being changed into a high-capital, low labor-cost industry in which individual employees will be highly paid and highly skilled. Passenger trains will probably need a human operator for many years if only to reassure passengers, but freight trains will probably run without anyone on board. Stations will need very few staff because ticket-selling and collecting will be entirely automatic and much of the present confusion of large stations will be eliminated by putting mail and luggage into small containers or pallets which can be loaded and unloaded swiftly by a mechanical truck. Parcels will probably have their own trains on busy routes and elsewhere they will be palletized. There will be fewer stations, and possibly passengers will be taken to and distributed from regional stations by road services—as they are to and from air terminals.

Bulk freight will travel in block trains, as much of it does today, but it is likely that coal traffic will be gradually reduced and eventually die out in many areas. The coal traffic that remains is likely to be between mine and industrial users, making for highly mechanized, swift and economical transport.

Short-range or commuter transport is likely to become still more important as the population increases and people tend more and more to gravitate toward urban areas, turning neighboring cities into giant urban conglomerates. The growth of purely urban or rapid transit lines can be taken for granted; the process of planning and building them is already well under way but what are now the suburban and outer suburban lines of the main line railroads are likely to undergo a change of some magnitude.

For shorter suburban trips, commuter trains are likely to become closer in design to those of rapid transit railroads.

Speed, space and comfort—the attributes of modern railroads.

Automobile transport, stacked
three high, in the United States.

Like them, they will probably be automatically driven with a
one-man crew, have a fairly small proportion of seats to
total capacity and plenty of standing space. Automatic
door operation is already in use on some suburban trains in
various parts of the world: it is likely to be adopted for all of
them. With increasing road congestion, stations on such lines
could well get nearer together making it possible for all commuters to walk to their local stations. This, in turn, could
lead to provision of express lanes on the railroads so that a
train could pick up passengers at neighboring stations and
then run as an express to the urban center. With modern signalling and the trend toward shorter but higher peaks, this type
of working might be possible by using both railroad tracks one

way on the tidal-flow principle, one track as the pick-up route and the other as the express, but this would only be possible if stabling space for trains were available at the center and trains did not have to make a swift return trip for another load of passengers. In such cases extra tracks would be needed. Passengers traveling in small numbers against the peak flow might even be catered to by road transport, with which the railway should have close liaison, including interchangeable tickets. Where a rapid transit railroad system exists there should be some through running of trains, as in Tokyo, which means there should be common loading gauges, common standards of current supply and automatic operating systems capable of controlling both types of train. Suburban lines would obviously need to be completely segregated from the high-speed main lines.

Some outer-suburban traffic, which even today can mean distances of up to 100 miles or so, could be put on the high-speed lines. The rest would be in comfortable trains with a high proportion of seats which would serve fairly widely spaced stations at first, switching to the fast suburban track at an interchange station on the edge of the inner suburban area and not calling at the closely spaced stations. Suburban stations could be one-or two-man operated and should serve as centers for feeder bus routes.

Careful thought will have to be given to the role of the bus in relation to railroads. Even now, as non-paying branch lines cease to operate, buses are taking their place. Just as buses feed urban railroad stations, so these longer-distance vehicles feed the main lines. But there are coaches which will pick the passenger up in his town and take him all the way to his destination much more cheaply, if more slowly, than the bus and train together. Good as railroad services may be, fares must also be watched very carefully.

Trains for Special Jobs

The role of the railroad in logistics has been discussed in an earlier chapter, but many of the trains involved in wars have been designed for purposes other than the carrying of troops and stores. During the last war many trains were used to carry tanks from manufacturers to depots. They were also used in the operational movement of squadrons and regiments of tanks from one front to another in Europe and in the movement of operational units from one area to another out of the line of battle. For such operational moves flat cars were used with bridge pieces covering the end gaps between cars. The tank squadron would drive straight on to the end of the train, much as automobiles do now, the leading tank going to the far end and the rest taking up positions along the train behind. The task of the leader, with the driver of the huge vehicle peering out through a small slit, was not enviable, and many tanks must have gone over the side or end of the train until the operation became familiar through practice.

Where military trains are moved through a conquered but still hostile countryside, or where raiding parties from the other side can be expected, the war-time railroad needs protection by constant patrol against sabotage or ambush. Even in the days of the African campaigns, the railroad that carried troops through the desert had trains headed by heavily armored cars that were pushed ahead of the locomotive and keeping a sharp watch for damaged track or enemies in waiting.

Similar heavily protected cars were used in the American Civil War, sometimes as patrol vehicles and sometimes as mobile blockhouses to guard bridges or other strategic points. In World War II German anti-sabotage measures in the occupied countries included armored trains which were virtually land battleships, swiveling gun turrets not excluded.

Massive cars have been used by several countries as bases for long-range guns, the only way to move these huge guns to their firing area being by rail. To prevent the enemy pinpointing them and destroying them by gunfire or bombing from the air, they were frequently moved to new positions, special sidings being built for them almost overnight. This role is now transferred to missiles, which are also mounted on suitable rail chassis. With the longer range of modern missiles the railroad is perhaps even more useful than before. Incidentally, the bombing raids of World War II showed quite clearly that it is a fallacy to think that a railroad can be knocked out for long by bombing only. Emergency repairs can be made very quickly. Once the right organization is set up, trains can be on their way again in a matter of hours after an ordinary attack.

Rockets are also used to propel vehicles on the fastest railroads in the world, the sledge tracks built in the United States to test ultrasonic aircraft and spacecraft equipment. There are quite a number of these, and they are true railroads, sometimes even of standard gauge, built to precision limits. The actual speeds reached are not disclosed, but the Supersonic Naval Ordnance Research Track (SNORT) at China Lake was

Armored train used in World War II for anti-sabotage patrols.

known to have held the world's land speed record until 1959 — what may have happened in recent years is anybody's guess. The sleds, carrying aircraft fuselages, parts of spacecraft, and so on, ride on metal shoes gliding on the top of the rail. To prevent the sled leaving the track there are small slippers which ride beneath the overhang of the rail head on each side. The sleds, having been rapidly accelerated by rockets up to high speed for the tests, are slowed down by running through shallow water or dragging a scoop through a water trough. The last two miles of the SNORT track can be flooded as required to various depths.

One of the disadvantages of railroads, as we have seen earlier, is that smooth steel wheels on smooth steel rails do not get a good enough grip to climb steep hills. Yet railroads do climb hills and climb more steeply than any road vehicle, given the right conditions.

The steepest gradient operated by unaided wheels (i.e. by adhesion alone) is 1 in 11 on the meter-gauge Chamonix line between Chedde and Servoz. This is an electrified line operated by the French National Railroad. To allow still steeper slopes to be climbed, a toothed wheel is fitted below the power car or locomotive of the train. The teeth on this wheel engage teeth cut into the edge of a metal bar, or rail, which is

fastened on edge between the running rails with the teeth upward. This gives a non-slip grip to the toothed wheel, which is driven by the motors of the train in the usual way. One of the most commonly used systems—it is used for the Pike's Peak line in the United States, the Snowdon Mountain Railroad in Britain and many Swiss mountain railroads—is the Abt, which has two toothed rails side-by-side but staggered so that the teeth of one come opposite the gaps in the other. There are also two toothed driving pinions, similarly staggered. In this way the grip is doubly secure as well as being smooth and constant. For the railroad up Mount Pilatus in Switzerland, which in places is as steep as 1 in 2, a special rack was devised by Dr. Locher, engineer of the line. There is a flat metal bar laid between the running rails with teeth cut in both sides, and the cars have pinions mounted in pairs with the rack rail between them. This not only gives a positive grip but also centers the cars on the track so that flanges on the running wheels are not necessary. This makes it easier for the cars to follow the very sharp curves on the line.

There are even steeper railroads, known as funiculars, on which the cars are hauled up by cables. There are usually two cars, one ascending and one descending, on opposite ends of the same cable so that the weight of one balances the other.

The U.S. Navy SNORT rocket sled track for aircraft testing.

This type of line can be worked by water power, the descending car having a large underfloor tank which is filled with water at the top of the slope to increase its weight, so that it can pull the other car up. The tank is emptied when the car reaches the bottom while the tank on the upper car is filled. Alternatively, the railroad can be worked by power winding mechanism. Such lines can be very steep indeed. One in Switzerland, between Piotta and Piora, climbs at 1 in $1\frac{1}{8}$, that is, the car moves 1 foot upward for every 1 foot $1\frac{1}{2}$ inches that it moves forward.

Montmartre funicular railroad
up the hill to the famous
Paris church of Sacré Coeur.

Monorails have been much in the news recently, although the first one was built as early as 1824 and had been patented three years before that. It seems almost a symbol of modernity among city planners to advocate a monorail system to carry passengers above the streets. Fortunately, the days when monorails were depicted as careening across the sky on a rail as thin as a piece of string, without any thought of weight, centrifugal force or even power supply, have gone. The monorails being presented as serious propositions today are sound engineering jobs depicted in a responsible way.

There are two main types of monorail contending for interest today. Neither of them is a true monorail in the sense of balancing above one rail —though such cars *have* been built in the past. The most successful monorail at present, in terms of lines built and working, is the Alweg. This is a supported

Electric rack locomotive pushing
its train up a mountain slope.

type, which means that the rail, which takes the form of a concrete beam on edge, is underneath the cars. The cars sit above the rail and are supported by rubber-tired driving wheels which run on the top edge of the beam. They are held upright and guided by horizontal rubber-tired wheels running on formed surfaces near the top and bottom of the beam sides. Along the 'web' of the beam, between the upper and lower tire tracks, is the power feed. There are Alweg-type lines—mostly short ones—in the United States and Japan, the latter with an eight-mile line between Tokyo and its airport which has shown the possibilities of this type of line for airport service. Because it is paralleled by a fast motorway, however, the line has been denied the financial success which had been hoped for it.

The other type of monorail, the French Safege, is somewhat different. The wheels, rubber-tired again, are mounted on bogies which run inside a box girder. The girder has a slit in the bottom surface through which pass supports for the car itself, which hangs below. This is a good example of the suspended monorail, though in fact the wheels run on surfaces on both sides of the slit in the girder so technically it is not a monorail. A trial line in France attracts many visitors.

Either supported or suspended monorails could be built down the center of wide streets high above the traffic. Some have been built in the past only to fade away, almost without trace. One which has not faded away is the suspended Wuppertal line in Germany, more than eight miles long, which has been working successfully since 1901. Built to solve a space problem in the narrow valley, it runs for much of its length above the River Wupper and for the rest above a main road.

A curious but very successful type of train running on the Spanish railroads is the 'Talgo', which is made up of small two-wheeled cars, the front of each being connected to the rear of the one ahead. The wheels are placed beneath the connected couplings. 'Talgo' comes from the words 'Train Articulé Léger Goicoechea et Oriel', the names being those of the inventor and his financial partner respectively. As is implied, the train is lightly built using aircraft and automobile techniques. In effect, the frames of the cars form a series of triangles that automatically follow one another as they are hauled along, so that the wheels are guided by the car ahead as well as by their flanges.

After extensive trials, the first Talgo train went into service

Alweg-type six-car monorail
train in Japan.

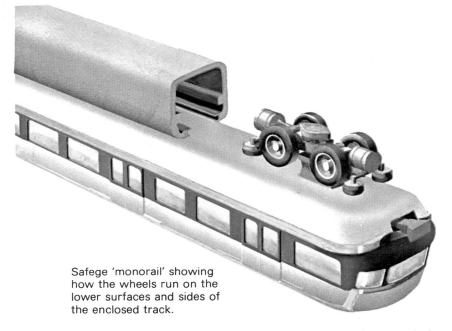

Safege 'monorail' showing
how the wheels run on the
lower surfaces and sides of
the enclosed track.

between Madrid and Hendaye in 1950. It proved particularly
suitable for this steeply graded run through the mountains
from the Spanish capital to the French frontier. Hauled by a
specially designed diesel locomotive, it cut the journey time
from almost twelve hours to under 8½. It also gave a high
standard of comfort, with meals served aircraft fashion at seats,
and air-conditioning. Though trials of a Talgo-type train in
the United States proved abortive, Spain has taken to the
Talgo and many of the country's best and fastest trains are
now of this type.

Finally, an automatic railroad whose cars have run more
than fifty million miles is the two-foot gauge Post Office
railroad in London. Opened in 1927, it has carried mails day
and night through its 6½ miles of deep tube tunnels ever since,
and all in trains which have no one on board to drive or super-
vise. The forty trains, the Post Office say, take the place of
1,700 trucks running on the congested London streets. To
avoid accidents, the cars, which run at up to 35 m.p.h.,
automatically cut off current from the section immediately
behind them. Special track circuiting stops them just before
they reach stations and brings them in at low speed. Brussels has a still smaller, seven-inch gauge automatic railroad

guided without having a railroad or conventional track to carry them. One of the principles they had in mind was to retain the easy rolling characteristics of the rail for the load but to use the friction produced by wheels running on a road. Thus we had systems like Larmanjat's, demonstrated in France from 1868 onward, in which the cars ran on a single rail with lateral support from road wheels, but the locomotive had its main driving wheels and weight on the road with subsidiary wheels only to steer it along the track. A modern version of this, designed by Major F. Dutton, was demonstrated at the Wembley British Empire Exhibitions of 1924–25. This had twin rail track on which the vehicles ran, but the tractor had wheels running on prepared strips outside the rails.

After this came systems in which all the vehicles ran on pneumatic tires but were guided by a single, non-load-carrying rail. One example of this was the 'Guideways' system tried out in India in the 1930's and subsequently refined and demonstrated as the 'Uniline' system in England in the 1950's. Very similar ideas, with detail differences, have been proposed for buses and airport services, in many cases with the added proposition that the vehicles should be capable of being steered so that they could also run on ordinary roads — a proposition put forward, incidentally, by Richard Trevithick in the earliest days of mechanical traction. An advantage of the guided system is that it can run on a track, or track

strips, just wide enough for its cars and will always follow an exact path, so that double-track paths can be provided with much less clearance than is needed on an ordinary road. The other advantage is that its vehicles can be joined up to run as a train operated by one or two men only. In essence, the Paris Metro rubber-tired vehicles are running on a guided road, though in this case the guidance is from side rails.

In recent years a new type of vehicle has been invented which has virtually no friction drag at all. It is known technically as a 'ground effect' vehicle. Though much of the United States development has been for use over water it is equally suitable for use over flat land and is potentially capable of high speeds. As at present under development, most ground effect vehicles, or cushion craft, depend on a fairly low-pressure cushion of air to keep them above the ground.

The idea now is to apply these craft to railroad purposes, using a smooth track which will give the best characteristics for the air cushion and at the same time provide

Model of high-speed monorail Levacar, with air-cushioned supporting and guiding slipper.

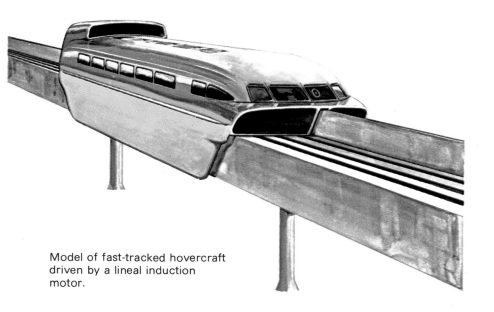

Model of fast-tracked hovercraft
driven by a lineal induction
motor.

precise guidance. An Englishman, Christopher Cockerell, is
generally regarded as the 'father' of the hovercraft, as this
type of vehicle is known in Great Britain. He has put forward
proposals for a tracked hovercraft which would seat 150 people
and run on special track shaped to fit the underside of the
vehicle, a half-inch air cushion giving the friction-free clearance
needed for the car. Trains of cars could be used at low speeds,
but for high speeds of up to 300 m.p.h. cars would run singly.
A twenty-mile track is being built, with British government
help, for high speed testing.

A somewhat similar scheme has been proposed by the Ford
company with its Levacar project. This would use air-
cushion vehicles running over prepared smooth surfaces —
possibly these would be twin surfaces looking like a conventional railroad — but using high air pressures of up to 100 p.s.i.
and having only a few thousandths of an inch clearance between rail and running gear. The principle is really more akin
to air-lubricated bearings than air cushioning. Propulsion, by
jet engines, would be at speeds of up to 500 m.p.h.

It is difficult to see how, in built-up countries, room could conveniently be found for long routes for either of these systems, but it might be possible to build them, at a price, above existing highways or railroads.

Yet another version of this idea has been tried very successfully in France. This is the Bertin aerotrain, which, in the prototype, has a small six-seat vehicle propelled by an aircraft engine. The concrete track is shaped like an inverted 'T', the base providing the flat surface needed by the air cushion and the central spine steering the car. The car can maneuver on rubber-tired wheels when off the track or use them on the track at low speeds when noise must be reduced. The Bertin car, with rocket assistance, has already attained a speed of 233 m.p.h. on a trial circuit near Paris. The project has the backing of the French government.

For vehicles of this type there is great promise in the linear induction motor now under development in several countries. Its principle is well known, and has been for many years, but efforts are now being directed to building it in a reasonably cheap but effective form. The linear motor is in effect a normal electric motor laid out flat, with the static part

of the motor producing a magnetic field which sweeps from one end to the other instead of moving around a circle as in an ordinary motor in which the field carries the rotor around with it. In the linear motor the 'rotor' is swept along in a straight line. When applied to a track, the 'rotor' portion can take the form of a steel or aluminum plate fixed permanently in position along the length of the whole track. There is no physical contact between one part of the motor and the other and no friction. The power applied is independent of contact between the vehicle and track, so that full power can be applied without the usual wheel slip.

It might seem that the linear motor is ideal for ordinary railroads with their lack of friction between wheel and rail, but experiments have shown that costs are much too high for low-speed work, and the linear motor does not come into its own below 150 m.p.h.

A possible alternative to an air cushion for frictionless movement is magnetic suspension, using repulsion magnets to lift a car a few inches. This has been suggested in the past but has been too expensive for any practical purpose, and

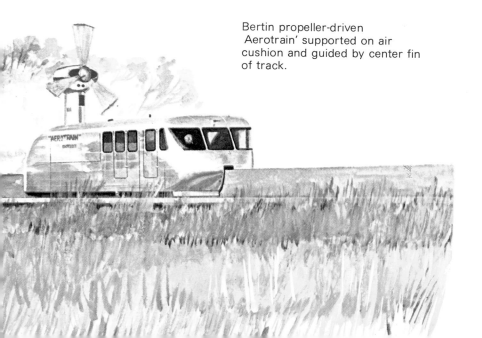

Bertin propeller-driven Aerotrain' supported on air cushion and guided by center fin of track.

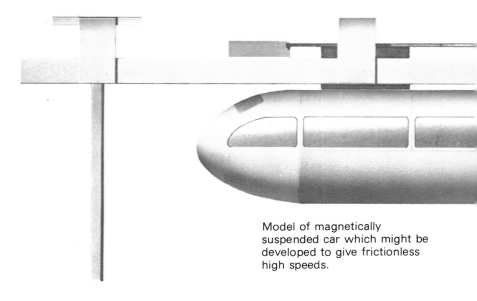

Model of magnetically
suspended car which might be
developed to give frictionless
high speeds.

electro-magnets have been essential. Now, with very powerful
permanent magnets available from the development of
ferrites, which are sintered ceramic materials based on ferric
oxide, it would be possible to install opposing magnets in the
track and in the car so as to achieve permanent flotation of the
car without using energy. Such a system is the 'Magnarail'
which would use magnets as described and propel the car by a
linear motor. Braking in linear motored vehicles is accom-
plished by reversing the motor, setting up a drag which
swiftly halts the car. In emergencies, cars could also drop
friction skids on to the track.

For transport in towns, a number of small-capacity systems
without rails have been suggested from time to time. One of
the first of these was the 'Never-Stop' railroad, which had no
rails but ran with rubber-tired wheels on two concrete strips.
They were steered by horizontal wheels running on the inside
edges of the strips and driven by a varying pitch spiral drive
running between the tracks. This was arranged with the
turns of the spiral closer together in stations, so that the
cars went through very slowly, giving plenty of time for
passengers to get in and out. Between stations the pitch

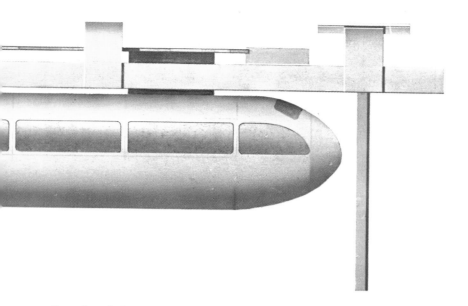

widened and the speed went up to 12 m.p.h. In more recent versions 36 m.p.h. can be reached. The 'Never-Stop' carried millions of people at the Wembley Exhibitions in England.

Among more recent systems is the 'staRRcar', or self-transit rail and road car. In this system the user can have the special small car overnight in his own garage. In the morning he drives off just as in a normal car until he reaches the nearest entrance to a staRRcar track. He enters this just as one would enter a highway, and once the car is on the track its driving is taken over automatically. As it enters the main track from the approach spur it speeds up to 70 m.p.h. until it reaches the rear of a train of staRRcars ahead, when it slows to 60 m.p.h. and joins the train, being joined in its turn by other cars behind. The driver then punches a code on buttons on the dash to show which exit from the staRRcar system he wishes to take. When the time comes his car is automatically switched out of the train on to a decelerating lane, at the end of which he drives off in the normal way. For those who cannot drive, a car could be picked up at a staRRcar garage connected to the system and routed to the garage nearest the destination. StaRRcar tracks would normally be over existing roads.

Running on a trial line in Pittsburgh are small Westinghouse Electric rubber-tired twenty-seat vehicles using a twin concrete surface track with a guide rail between. They are entirely automatic in operation and are controlled by a central computer. In slack hours they run singly but in peak hours can form trains of up to ten cars. These attractive vehicles are capable of 50 m.p.h. between stations. Variously called 'Skybus' or 'Transit Expressway' it is regarded as a promising low-cost rapid transit system for cities of medium size. This system, with two other developments, earned for Westinghouse the United States Department of Housing and Urban Development's first award for outstanding achievement in urban transportation development. It has been adopted for the Tampa airport and is likely to be used in Baltimore for at least one rapid transit route.

For the last century and a half, railroads have risen, flourished and now are apparently declining. But before railroads

'Skybus' rubber-tired rail-guided
unmanned urban
train on trials in Pittsburgh,
Pennsylvania.

die, it is likely they will develop to yet unsuspected heights. They may well have another century or more of life before them. The economic magic of steel wheels on steel rails still holds good. The new fast passenger and freight trains and the tremendous upsurge in urban mass transit testify to this. However, there will be many changes. The new technologies may leave little of the traditional features of railroads, perhaps no more than their self-guiding characteristics. If the methods prove superior, it is proper that rails should give way to them. It should not be forgotten that railroads exist to carry passengers and goods and not as an end in themselves. In any event, the new railroads will be a far cry from those fledgling mining railroads of the early 19th century.

'You are not the same people who left that station
Or who will arrive at any terminus,
While the narrowing rails slide together behind you.'

T. S. Eliot

MUSEUMS TO VISIT

This list is not comprehensive. There are many museums with transport exhibits in the United States and visitors should make inquiries locally.

The Smithsonian Institution, Washington, D.C.
Chicago Museum of Science and Industry, Chicago, Illinois.
Colorado Railroad Museum, Golden, Colorado.
Ohio Railway Museum, Worthington, Ohio.
Henry Ford Museum, Dearborn, Michigan.
Museum of Transport, St. Louis, Missouri.
'Steamtown U.S.A.', North Walpole, New Hampshire.
Benjamin Franklin Institute, Philadelphia, Pennsylvania.
Railroad Museum, Jackson, Tennessee.

The publishers wish to thank Faber and Faber Ltd. and Harcourt, Brace & World, Inc. for permission to reprint the lines that appear on page 155 from T. S. Eliot's 'The Dry Salvages' from *The Four Quartets*.

BOOKS TO READ

The Robber Barons. Matthew Josephson. Harcourt, 1934.

The Railroads of the South. John F. Stover. University of North Carolina Press, 1955.

Hear the Train Blow: A Pictorial Epic of America in the Railroad Age. Lucius Beebe and Charles Clegg. Grosset & Dunlap, 1952.

Casey Jones' Locker. Frederic J. Shaw. Hisperian House, 1959.

The Twilight of Steam Locomotives. Ron Ziel. Grosset & Dunlap, 1963.

Mansions on Wheels — the Private Railway Car. Howell-North, 1959.

To Hell in a Day Coach. Peter Lyon. Lippincott, 1968.

Moguls and Iron Men: history of the first transcontinental railroad. James McCaque. Harper, 1964.

American Railroads. John F. Stover. University of Chicago Press, 1961.

Focus: the Railroad in Transition. Robert S. Carper. A. S. Barnes, 1968.

Outlook for Railroads. Poyatz Tyler (ed.). H. M. Wilson, 1960.

The Railroad Station — an architectural history. Carroll Louis Vander-glice Meeks. Yale University Press, 1956.

The Railway Age. Michael Robbins. Penguin, 1965.

Unusual Railways. John R. Day and B. G. Wilson. Macmillan, 1960.

More Unusual Railways. John R. Day. Macmillan, 1960.

INDEX

159